AGAINST FREUD

Critics Talk Back

Todd Dufresne

STANFORD UNIVERSITY PRESS

STANFORD, CALIFORNIA

2007

Stanford University Press

Stanford, California

©2007 by the Board of Trustees of the Leland Stanford Junior University. All
rights reserved.

Printed in the United States of America on acid-free, archival-quality paper

Library of Congress Cataloging-in-Publication Data

Against Freud : critics talk back / [edited by] Todd Dufresne.

   p. cm.

 Includes bibliographical references and index.

  ISBN 978-0-8047-5547-4 (cloth : alk. paper) -- ISBN 978-0-8047-5548-1 (pbk. :
alk. paper)

 1. Freud, Sigmund, 1856-1939. 2. Psychoanalysis. I. Dufresne, Todd, 1966-

BF109.F74A52 2007

150.19'52092--dc22   2006102116

Typeset by Bruce Lundquist in 11/13.5 Garamond

*This book is dedicated to all the people with whom
I've happily argued the night away, beginning with my father,
Raymond Dufresne, who is missed.*

Contents

Preface

The figures interviewed for *Against Freud* are well known for their contributions to Freud scholarship. They include a pioneer psychiatrist, a clinical psychologist and pioneer psychoanalyst, a literary critic, a trained sociologist, a physics teacher, two historians, and three philosophers. Each has earned a reputation as a staunch critic of Freud and psychoanalysis. Each has published significant works, some of them classics, on the subject of psychoanalysis. And each, at some point in his or her career, has been reviled by some and lionized by others. All, I submit, have something important to say about psychoanalysis, roughly one century after its creation (ca. 1897–1900).

Against Freud is designed for two primary audiences. First and foremost, it is designed for interested lay readers. Why? Because the pace of Freud scholarship has made it nearly impossible for anyone but the most dedicated scholar to keep up with current thinking about the state of psychoanalysis. Moreover, given the volume of works published annually combined with the presence of sometimes-hidden agendas, lay readers barely know where to begin or, more frankly, who to trust. Arguably, in no academic field is such a high degree of suspicion, contempt, and disagreement—in short, distrust—more apparent than in Freud studies. It is certainly a peculiar situation for a theory and practice that Freud believed was based on objectively true scientific discoveries. Yet controversy and division were probably inevitable, given the different interests involved. On one side are the clinicians, themselves divided along strict and often mutually exclusive party lines, who as a group are the least likely to care about the coherence of psychoanalytic ideas. On the other side are the academics and theorists, themselves divided according to disciplinary and intellectual norms, who as a group are the least likely to care about everyday concerns about therapy. Between them run the gamut of interested participants, from middle- and upper-middle-class analysands, who visit psychoanalysts for help with their life problems, to all variety of artists, who, sometimes willy-nilly, incorporate psychoanalytic ideas into their works.

By providing a venue for some of Freud's most prominent and aggressive critics of the last thirty-five years, this book provides a foundation on which lay readers can build their own ideas and opinions about Freud, psychoanalysis, and contemporary criticism. *Against Freud* is organized around a central theme: the decline of psychoanalysis in the late twentieth century. This theme has the great merit of providing new and occasional readers of Freud the chance to understand things from an overt and coherent perspective. Moreover, this critical approach to psychoanalytic culture is valuable for its own sake. Because despite a decade of media interest in the "death of psychoanalysis," the truth is that most psychoanalytic literature remains pro-Freudian in crucial ways. Freud is still very much with us, and not just in the mundane use of clever ideas such as penis envy and anal character. Vested interests run deep, informing social policy and entire worldviews, making this kind of book not just useful but absolutely necessary.

So what kind of book is this? Nowhere else will you find a book devoted to the frank musings of prominent critics of psychoanalysis. And nowhere will you find a more immediately accessible and coherent discussion about the problems in, and limitations of, psychoanalysis. Beginners in psychoanalysis and interested lay readers will certainly find this material invaluable if they are inclined to make informed decisions about Freud's work and legacy.

Second and perhaps surprisingly, this book is designed for writers and scholars who dabble in psychoanalysis without knowing much about its inner debates and multiple complexities. Self-styled *bricoleurs* and interdisciplinary scholars often have a tough time with the field of psychoanalysis, which is already so thoroughly cross-disciplinary that confusion has always been the norm, not the exception. Think about it: just as Freud himself sampled widely from literature, philosophy, neurology, natural science, mythology, medical hypnosis, and more, theorists after him threw into the mix other ideas borrowed from surrealism, phenomenology, hermeneutics, Marxism, cybernetics, structuralism, poststructuralism, and mathematics. As a result, readers are routinely baffled by a field that defies understanding, even among those who make it their life's work. *Against Freud* provides the much-needed inside story, and occasionally some dirt, about the theory, practice, and business of psychoanalysis across a range of critical perspectives and specialities. I submit that even sophisticated readers will appreciate the collective insights of such a knowledgeable group.

In fact, by listening in on conversations with Freud's most informed and aggressive critics, we can all learn more about this truly difficult but always fascinating field of study. Questions are posed, issues are discussed, and risks are taken. What was it like for the psychiatrist Joseph Wortis to be analyzed by Freud himself? To what extent does Marxism influence Wortis's thinking? According to Esther Menaker, herself trained as a psychoanalyst in Freud's Vienna, what kind of analyst was Freud's daughter, Anna? What good is child analysis anyway? According to the historian of medicine Edward Shorter, is psychoanalysis a form of medical malpractice? How did Shorter land himself in hot water when he emphasized the Jewish milieu in which Freud lived and worked? Does the historian of science Frank Sulloway think that psychoanalysis is a pseudoscience, a religion, or both? What role has the legend of Freud played in the transmission of psychoanalysis? How did literary critic Frederick Crews get interested in Freud? What does he think are the essential mistakes of psychoanalysis? After posing the question "Was Freud a Liar?" in 1973, does the philosopher Frank Cioffi now believe that Freud in fact dissembled? Why does he now think that Karl Popper's doctrine of falsification is not the best way to understand the limitations of psychoanalysis? How did Allen Esterson, who studied and taught physics, ever get involved with psychoanalysis? What did Freud's seminal case studies teach Esterson about Freud and psychoanalysis? Does Han Israëls really believe that the field of Freud studies is overrun with psychopathic personalities? Why is he fed up with debate over Freud's famous seduction theory? Why is French philosopher Mikkel Borch-Jacobsen so interested in the history of suggestion and hypnosis? Since his days as a deconstructionist, has he become a naive positivist or, perhaps worse, an intemperate Freud basher? Why, according to me, are so many bad books written on psychoanalysis? What do I have to say about the relationship between psychoanalysis and contemporary literary and cultural theory?

The following interviews provide answers to pressing questions about Freud's life, work, and enduring legacy. As befits real conversations with experts in the field, they are by turns serious, chatty, funny, contentious, lighthearted, seditious, informative, and, above all, teacherly. The reader gets a real taste of the personalities involved, their likes and dislikes, and their ways of thinking, and will find that, while these critics of psychoanalysis are in broad agreement about Freud and psychoanalysis, they are by no means a homogeneous bunch. I submit that there is no better introduction to their thought than by hearing what it is they have to say about their own work, even as they unpack what they see as the essential problems in psychoanalysis.

Naturally, the interviews have been edited for repetition, flow, simple errors, and overall coherence. Whenever possible the interviewee has had an opportunity to qualify his or her words, adding to some statements and removing others. These features are hardly limitations, however, since each interview was explicitly intended, if not designed, to be recorded, transcribed, and edited for future readers. The editing means that some of the normal idiosyncrasies of speech—hums and haws and false starts—have been removed for the sake of readers. Although such editing is entirely typical of interviews, especially with academics, it should nonetheless be acknowledged.

The interviews were originally conducted by me; two like-minded colleagues, Mikkel Borch-Jacobsen and Sonu Shamdasani; and my friend and colleague, the Toronto gestalt therapist Antonio Greco. When appropriate, some interviews were updated in 2005. That said, I alone am responsible for selecting and editing the final product. Finally, a word about the inclusion of an interview conducted with me by Greco. This interview, included at the urging of my editor, presents an opportunity for readers to know better the views of the person responsible for editing and selecting content for this book. Transparency is at the heart of criticism, and it begins with me. But I also hope that my discussion about postmodernism widens the scope of the book, which after all touches on many facets of the contemporary reception of Freud and psychoanalysis. I hasten to add that, while this interview closes the book, its placement says nothing about the evolution of Freud criticism from, say, Wortis to me. It is rather meant to suggest that skepticism about the role of Freud and contemporary theory is in short supply. In this respect, *Against Freud* ends with a live provocation and an indication of debates to come.

· · ·

Against Freud opens with an economical introduction on the life and work of Sigmund Freud, written not from the perspective of filial piety but from the perspective of current Freud criticism. Because of decades of misinformation and myth-building, this perspective is sometimes called the "revisionist" reading of Freud. Others prefer, more simply, to call it the true—or, at any rate, the less-false—reading of Freud. The idea here is to clear a space for thought to begin about psychoanalysis, a field that almost everyone assumes they know something about—whether it is the theories of repression, free association, and the Oedipus complex, or the practice of lying on a couch and talking—even though they often aren't sure if what they know is actually true or how what they know fits, or doesn't fit, with what Freud himself thought. This introduction will hopefully put us all on the same footing as we begin to listen in on the discussions that follow.

I have also included a short suggested reading section on useful books and articles on the subject of psychoanalysis. Interested readers of *Against Freud* may find, in the end, that they want more details about Freud criticism. First, however, they may want to obtain some direction on the classic secondary texts of Freud studies and to read what advocates of psychoanalysis think about its purported decline. Needless to say, many people disagree with the critical views collected here, citing either the tone or substance of one argument or another. But actually, perhaps unsurprisingly, there is no consensus in this respect. A partisan of psychoanalysis will often agree with many of the criticisms collected here but will nonetheless take a stand on a particular issue or set of issues. Another partisan will defend an entirely different issue or set of issues. Taken together, as Crews and others have pointed out, the partisan commentators grant legitimacy to nearly all the claims made by the different critics. The shorthand for this process of division, not only between proponents and opponents of Freud but also within their ranks, is called the Freud wars—itself a fairly complex subset of the so-called culture wars, at least in the United States. Readers are well advised to keep this conflict in mind as they listen to critics do their best to convince them that psychoanalysis died long before the "psychoanalytic century" actually ended. That I agree with them obviously doesn't mean they are right. It is up to you to read them and decide for yourself, which is precisely the raison d'être of this book.

ACKNOWLEDGMENTS

This project depended entirely on the trust and goodwill of everyone involved. The critics I interviewed, or contacted for revisions in 2005, were unfailingly generous, even when we disagreed, and demonstrated by example what it means to be part of a community of scholars, however "pathological" that community may be. I am in their considerable debt, personally and intellectually. I'd also like to acknowledge particular help or inspiration I received along the way. Paul Roazen's own interview work in the 1960s first inspired me to undertake this project in the early 1990s. He also gave me the contact information for Joseph Wortis and Esther Menaker. Clara Sacchetti was often a traveling companion and was a sounding board during and after research trips. Mikkel Borch-Jacobsen took time out of a busy trip to Toronto for food, work, and questions; then, in 2005, he and Sonu Shamdasani provided access to their own interviews. Frederick and Betty Crews generously put me up in their Berkeley home and indulged me as a guest. Michael Shermer helped me formulate better questions for Crews, provided a perfect venue for the interview at *Skeptic*, and encouraged its reproduction here. Frank Cioffi came in from Canterbury to meet with me and Esterson in London, and then almost missed his train home. Frank Sulloway answered all my e-mail queries quickly and without complaint, even when he was on a research trip in the Galápagos. Justin Wintle originally asked me to write about Freud's life and work for his book, *New Makers of Modern Culture*, and then generously encouraged me to reproduce my efforts here. Sonu Shamdasani provided me with electronic copies of the interviews with Israëls, Sulloway, and others. A very special thanks to Norris Pope at Stanford University Press, who originally encouraged me to collect and improve the interviews for this book, and to Carolyn Brown, who kept it all on track, and Alison Rainey, who provided expert copyediting. Heartfelt cheers to everyone.

Parts of this book have appeared before in English, and I am grateful for permission to reproduce them here. The introduction appeared as

"Sigmund Freud, 1856–1939" in *New Makers of Modern Culture*, edited by Justin Wintle (London: Routledge, 2007: 524–28). The Wortis interview appeared as "An Interview with Joseph Wortis" in the *Psychoanalytic Review* 83, no. 4, August 1996: 589–607, and is reprinted with permission of the Guilford Press. The Crews interview appeared as "The Making of a Freud Skeptic: An Interview with Frederick Crews" in *Skeptic* 7, no. 3, 1999: 42–49. The interview is reprinted with permission of the Guilford Press. A version of the Dufresne interview by Antonio Greco appeared as "Psychoanalysis, Parasites, and the 'Culture of Banality'" in *Killing Freud: Twentieth-Century Culture and the Death of Psychoanalysis* by T. Dufresne (London: Continuum, 2003) and is reprinted with permission of the Continuum International Publishing Group.

I am also happy to acknowledge the support I've had from my friends and colleagues at Lakehead University and in Thunder Bay, especially Bruce Muirhead, Sandi Bair, Ron Harpelle, Kelly Saxberg, Chris Southcott, Laura Hope-Southcott, Tom Dunk, Bonnie Nistico, Marc Bode, Christine Bode, Richard Berg, Eric Niemi, Jill Konkin, Tim Zmijowskyj, and Gillian Siddall. Other sources of long-term support include Paul Antze, Rodolphe Gasché, and my old friend Tony Greco.

I'd also like to thank my family for their support, personal as well as intellectual. Thanks especially to the Dufresnes—Raymond, Jacquie, Guy, Wendy, Sarah, and Mattie. Thanks also to Bob Magnusson and Bob Bulger and to the Sacchettis, Maria and Attilio. Clara Sacchetti still makes it all possible, tolerating more discussions about Freud and company than she could possibly want. And then there is our daughter, Chloe, who helps me set it all aside for another day. Thanks.

Finally, I am also happy to recognize the financial support I have received over the years from the Social Sciences and Humanities Research Council of Canada for travel and other expenses associated with this and related projects. I appreciate it.

Todd Dufresne
November 2006

AGAINST FREUD

Introduction:

The Revised Life and Work of Sigmund Freud

Sigmund Freud was born on May 6, 1856, in Moravia, the present-day Czech Republic, and relocated with his family to Vienna, Austria, four years later. He remained there for most of his life, becoming world famous for creating psychoanalysis and for establishing psychotherapy more generally in the Western world. Freud and his immediate family did not flee Nazi-controlled Austria until 1938, only a year before his death. After a lengthy battle with cancer of the jaw, Freud died in north London, England, on September 23, 1939.

The young Freud, a polyglot, was a gifted student who excelled in his studies. First he imagined for himself a career in politics or the law, and then in science, in particular in the field of neurology. At the University of Vienna, Freud stretched out his studies from five years to eight, taking personal interest courses in philosophy and conducting extensive laboratory research. For example, under the direction of Carl Claus and his Institute of Comparative Anatomy, in 1875 Freud dissected and examined under microscope the testes of four hundred eels. And in 1876 Freud began a six-year stint as a researcher under Ernst Brücke at the Institute of Physiology. There he worked on the spinal cords of the brook lamprey, the nerve cells of the crayfish, and the nervous system of the freshwater crab. On a holiday in 1878 the very keen young man also conducted research on the salivary glands of dogs in Salomon Strickler's experimental pathology laboratory. Finally, in 1881, Freud took his examinations for the doctor of medicine degree, after which time he put in another three years of residency at the Vienna General Hospital.

Freud continued to conduct research at the hospital. In 1883 he worked with Theodor Meynert in the hospital's psychiatry department and took up neuroanatomy, eventually publishing articles in the field. Then, in 1884, Freud began his infamous studies of cocaine, a drug he used himself, promoted to friends and professional colleagues, and published gushing reports about.

A year later Freud became lecturer in neuropathology at the University of Vienna, and in that capacity won a grant to study at the Salpêtrière in Paris with the famous neurologist, Jean-Martin Charcot. There he studied hysteria and hypnosis with the man he always considered his master. Advancement as a university researcher, however, was largely barred to even secular Jews who, like Freud, refused to convert to Christianity. So in 1886, freshly married to Martha Bernays, Freud the neurologist reluctantly embarked on a career treating "nervous" illness. But he never abandoned his dream of becoming a recognized scientist and from the beginning viewed clinical practice as laboratory research by another name.

During the so-called prepsychoanalytic period of research, roughly 1887–1897, Freud sought to bridge the fields of neurophysiology and psychology. Often exchanging new speculations with his close friend Wilhelm Fliess, the Berlin ear, nose, and throat specialist, Freud wrote *The Project for a Scientific Psychology* in 1895. Invoking nineteenth-century science and speculative nature philosophy, Freud postulated ideas that would influence him, at first covertly and then explicitly, for a lifetime. That Freud never completed or published the *Project* does not mean that he forgot it. On the contrary, many ideas first introduced there return in his late texts. For example, the early and late Freud argued that repetitive behaviors once associated with railway and war traumas can be explained by invoking the theory of recapitulation and the inheritance of acquired characteristics; that existence itself is determined, if not undercut, by the theory of constancy (or entropy), the idea that all living systems seek rest as their natural state; that emotional trauma can be explained in quantitative or economic terms as the overflowing of affect into the interior of a delicate psyche; and, more generally, that life is governed by reality and pleasure principles.

From the prepsychoanalytic period Freud is better known for his contribution to *Studies on Hysteria* (1895). Freud had lobbied a very reluctant

Josef Breuer, a mentor and well-regarded Viennese physician, to collaborate on this book, which is remembered for the theoretical claims that strangulated affect causes hysteria; that talking is efficacious; and, more incredibly, that through such talk one can uncover layers of repressed memories leading back to some sexually charged traumatic event or "seduction." Freud essentially came to believe that these memories were buried underneath the defensive mechanisms of the psyche and that psychology, like the exciting and relatively new science of archaeology, needed new methods and theories with which to reveal them.

Freud and Breuer's sophisticated critics of that time were not convinced. Above all, they warned that the repeated, recovered, or abreacted memories central to the "talking cure" were almost certainly artifacts of the method; the critics pointed to Charcot, whose reputation for inducing patient compliance was settled by the time of his death in 1893, and to the history of medical hypnosis to make their case. Freud, characteristically, rejected their warnings even though he privately began to realize that the patient "memories" he had reported were indeed false. Freud faced a crisis—his published findings were in fact wrong and his reputation, already compromised by his advocacy of cocaine, could now be ruined. His response to this crisis was nothing less than the creation of psychoanalysis proper.

Although problematic, Freud's own retrospective accounts of the abandonment of the seduction theory and birth of psychoanalysis are clear. What Freud had already called psychoanalysis in 1896 was after 1897 reconceived as the analysis of the emotional rapport, or transference, between patient and physician. Moreover, this rapport was now understood to be infused with sexual fantasy, itself a repetition of inner turmoil based on unresolved, repressed, and unconscious sexual conflicts. Freud claimed to have dropped hypnosis altogether from his practice, thus supposedly evading the problem of suggestion and of discovering the ubiquity of childhood sexuality and the doctrine of polymorphous perversity. His revised claim: hysteria and the neuroses are psychologically conditioned and are not caused by sexual abuse. And so while Freud had been fundamentally right to dig deep for some repressed and unconscious meaning at the heart of mental illness, he was wrong to have accepted the reports of his early patients. He had mistaken their fantasies of abuse for actual abuse.

Never again would Freud risk the future of his science, and of his reputation, on the objective (and therefore verifiable) reality of past events.

At its best, psychoanalysis took refuge in the fantasy life of the individual neurotic, if not in the self-analysis of Freud's own dreams and neuroses, which were not just objectively knowable but were in principle universally true of all people and cultures. At its worst, psychoanalysis dictated the conclusions it purported to find, brazenly manipulating case studies to reflect the ever-changing theoretical and political exigencies of the day. Such was the case of Anna O. We now know that this patient, Bertha Pappenheim, not only failed to recover from hysteria, as claimed, but also was addicted to morphine at the end of her treatment with Breuer and institutionalized in a Swiss sanatorium. Her new doctor's surprising diagnosis: hysteria. A year later Breuer confided that he wished Pappenheim would die so she would be released from suffering. Yet, at Freud's urging, they presented this utter failure of the talking cure as the foundation of the *Studies on Hysteria*.

Psychoanalytic methodology is no less a quagmire than its theory. Freud failed to say exactly what psychoanalysis was until years after its birth, publishing his "Papers on Technique" between 1911 and 1915. Until the *Three Essays on the Theory of Sexuality* of 1905, readers were left to assume that by psychoanalysis Freud still meant the recovery of actual memories of childhood sexual abuse. In other words, although Freud dropped the seduction etiology in a private letter to Fliess in 1897, readers wouldn't know this for another eight years. Freud kept busy just the same, publishing works of "psychoanalysis"—most notably his lengthy self-analysis, conducted in the wake of his father's death in 1896, *The Interpretation of Dreams* (1900).

Later on Freud would claim that his early work had been routinely ignored or misunderstood, and he wouldn't shrink from diagnosing the cause of this apparent resistance on the part of society and of his critics. This was the time of his self-mythologized "splendid isolation." But Freud's attitude was merely a romantic pose, a retrospective fiction behind which he spun his own legend, since he was hardly ignored in his own time. On the strength of his publications and the claims of efficacy drawn therein, in 1902 Freud was able to gather around himself a small group of loyal adherents for "Wednesday Evening Meetings," precursor of the Vienna Psychoanalytic Society of 1906–1915. This diverse group met weekly to discuss Freud's work and learn about psychoanalysis from the master himself. Indeed, these meetings were the primary activity required of people wanting to become analysts in the early days.

In 1907 Freud's fortunes brightened further when the Swiss psychiatrist Carl Jung became a follower. Not only would Jung's involvement bring psychoanalysis into contact with a respected research institute and discipline but it would take analysis out of the Jewish milieu in which Freud and his adherents, themselves largely Jewish, lived and practiced. In other words, Jung's very presence would lend weight to the claim that psychoanalysis was a science.

Jung did his part to advance psychoanalysis as a theory and movement. For example, it was Jung who introduced Freud to the Zurich experiments in word association, which became a core idea of psychoanalytic practice. Freud soon required his patients to "free associate," that is, to speak freely about whatever ideas popped into their heads, often in relation to a dream or fantasy. Jung also championed more institutional rigor among those who called themselves Freudians, arguing that all prospective analysts should be analyzed, an idea that would soon become a key feature of institutional psychoanalysis.

As in his past relationships with Fliess and Breuer, however, Freud demanded strict adherence to his ideas and was intolerant when anyone wavered on key points of doctrine or turned psychoanalysis against him. And so Freud, although once desperate see Jung as his successor, broke with him in 1912. Freud's *Totem and Taboo* (1913), a fantastical work about the prehistorical origin of guilt and conscience in a presumed act of parricide, would be the first in a series of blows and counterblows between the two men.

Psychoanalysis nonetheless prospered. By this time those in the field were developing their own journals, publishing house, and training institutions, and enjoyed a growing international presence. Well-placed Freudians included Ernest Jones in London, Karl Abraham in Berlin, Sandor Ferenczi in Budapest, and Otto Rank in Vienna. When World War I came along, psychoanalysis quickly spread as a possible method for treating intractable war traumas and neuroses. In turn, medically trained followers increasingly surrounded Freud and a core group of disciples, the self-anointed "secret committee," who together established psychoanalysis throughout the Western world.

In the midst of this upswing, Freud, recommitting himself to the dualism he always favored, announced in *Beyond the Pleasure Principle* (1920) that the theory of sexual fantasy needed a counterpart, a theory of the death drive. But few of Freud's adherents shared his breadth of learning or intellectual curiosity, and not many of them accepted this new view. Fewer yet understood why he would complicate a perfectly good, and by then well accepted, theory of sexuality. To explain *Beyond,* some pointed to Freud's well-known pessimism and misanthropy; the death of a favorite daughter; the events of World War I, in which two sons served; unresolved emotional conflicts; and even boredom during the interwar period.

Even now insufficient attention is given to the connection between Freud's new "metapsychology" of 1915–1920—of which the death drive theory is the crowning achievement—and the oldest prepsychoanalytic ideas of the 1880s and 1890s. But once the connection is made one cannot ignore the entirely wrongheaded aspects of Freud's scientific worldview, including the intricate biologism that underwrites the enterprise. For example, in the wake of the rediscovery of Mendelian genetics in 1900, few serious scientists could believe in the inheritance of acquired characteristics. Freud did, however, figuring this lack of belief was a problem for others. As he plainly admits in *Moses and Monotheism* (1939), much to the embarrassment of his followers, "I cannot do without this factor [i.e., Lamarkian inheritance] in biological evolution."

Freud's retrograde biologism is even more ironic in that his final "cultural" works, all made possible by his biologically determined theory of the death drive, are now considered among his most famous and classic. This includes *The Future of an Illusion* of 1927, in which he reduces religion to an infantile attachment to Daddy, and *Civilization and Its Discontents* of 1930, in which he analyzes the persistent discomforts of civilized existence. Similarly, clinicians especially have not well appreciated that Freud's late turn toward ego psychology in *The Ego and the Id* (1923)—and along with it the shift from the conscious/unconscious model of mental functioning to that of the famous superego/ego/id—was conditioned by this old biologism. Unfortunately, Freud's explicit biological statements in these late works have been downplayed or simply ignored in favor of his more acceptable, if more trite, conclusions about the repressed, guilt-ridden individual of modern society. According to the sanitized view of Freud's late work, society often requires too much repression and deferred satisfaction of individuals. To compensate, the lucky few sublimate their discomfort with civilization into art and science, while the mob is consigned to infantile submission to God, neuroses, or both. Freud's vision is actually darker and more complex. He perversely claimed that human beings are driven to death by biology, one acquired and inherited over millennia. Consequently, the shape of human achievement—art, science, religion—is an aberration, however glorious, along a path to nonexistence. The upshot: psychoanalysis can do very little about our historically inevitable, biologically acquired neuroses. As he said in 1927, human progress is best measured not in hours, months, or even years, but in geological time. Psychoanalysis is therefore *unendlich*, or "interminable," as Freud admitted in 1937, thus putting the unmistakable stamp of therapeutic pessimism on the entire endeavor.

After his death in 1939 Freud's influence continued to spread throughout Western society, from medicine, psychiatry, and psychotherapy to literature, criticism, philosophy, and, more generally, postmodernism. A medicalized psychoanalysis prospered in the United States, at least until the late 1960s, whereas a more humanities-based psychoanalysis flourished in the 1970s and, energized by such French theorists as Jacques Lacan and Jacques Derrida, spread throughout the Western world. But today, after the advent of drug therapies and the decline of postmodern theory, psychoanalysis seems to have run its course. Naturally Freud remains one of the undisputed giants of twentieth-century thought. But his legacy has been radically undermined as critics continue to debate the scientific foundations of his work, including the theories of repression and of the unconscious; his clinical method, or lack thereof; the efficacy of his practice and of therapeutic talk in general; the ethics of his life and work; and the internecine politics of the psychoanalytic movement. Indeed, aside from motivated holdouts with reputations to lose, it is now widely believed that psychoanalysis as a viable theory and practice is dead or dying.

"The Man Who Was Analyzed by Freud":
Joseph Wortis on Freud, Freudians,
and Social Justice

Interviewed by Todd Dufresne

Dr. Joseph Wortis first majored in English but then switched to a premedical track before he received a degree from New York University in 1927. Afterward he studied medicine in Vienna, Munich, and Paris, graduating from the Medical Faculty of the University of Vienna in 1932. With the support of the sexologist Havelock Ellis and the psychiatrist Adolph Meyer, Wortis received a generous research fellowship in psychiatry with the understanding that he would later focus on sex and homosexuality. Because his mandate was broad, he arranged an analysis with Sigmund Freud. To this end, a sum of $1,600 was made available, and Freud agreed to analyze Wortis until that amount was spent: twenty dollars per hour, five times a week, for sixteen weeks. The analysis took place between October 1934 and January 1935, when Wortis and Freud were 28 and 76 years old, respectively.

At one point in the interview the phone rang and Wortis told his caller: "I have a graduate student from Canada who is seeing me in my now well-established role as The Man Who Was Analyzed by Freud [*hearty laughter*]. It's an irony that a notorious antipsychoanalyst like me should achieve a reputation as The Man Who Was Analyzed by Freud." As it happens, many historians of psychoanalysis have needed the past forty years to catch up with some of the sentiments expressed in Wortis's book, *Fragments of an Analysis with Freud*, published in 1954.

I interviewed Wortis on February 26, 1994, in his cluttered Brooklyn office on Hicks Street, in a house where he had lived for over fifty years. He was active, lucid, and intellectually engaging. At that time he was 87 and was one of the last of Freud's analysands still living. He died one year later.

. . .

TD: Could you tell me something about your family background?

JW: My mother was French, and my father was Russian born. They were both Jewish, but they were deeply embedded in their respective ancestral cultures. I guess in my father's case it was Yiddish; of course, the Russian Jewish communities were rather isolated. But in my mother's case, I regard her as profoundly French. All of her relatives here were very French. They looked upon people of my father's background as strange foreigners. I was raised in an Italian and Polish immigrant neighborhood in Brooklyn, surrounded by schoolmates who came from immigrant families. The public school I attended had mostly children of Polish and Italian immigrants. I came from one of the few families where English was spoken, because the only language my parents could use to communicate with each other was English. My parents, though they had little formal education, were quite intellectual and, in their own way, cultured. My father was very musical and my mother read constantly in three languages—French, German, and English—and had us start reading when we were toddlers. I think it was largely under this influence that I became an intellectual. On the one hand, I felt very indigenous American, and have a great love for the English language. On the other hand, I was exposed to all of these cultures, not only in terms of the people around me, people who visited my home, my relatives and so on, but also because I studied abroad.

TD: Were you raised in a Jewish atmosphere?

JW: I was raised as an orthodox atheist. I had no religious feeling whatsoever because of my background and also because of the ideology on my father's side of the family, which was socialist. In fact, a cousin of mine was one of the founders of the Communist Party, and they were all thorough atheists. So I had no religious identification, and because of the neighborhood I grew up in and because of my parents' background, I had very little ethnic identification.

TD: This, I think, comes across in your dealings with Freud.

JW: I think I drew Freud out a little bit on the Jewish question. I also remember expressing some anti-Semitic ideas. Well, why is a Jew anti-Semitic? First of all I had no identification with the bulk of the Jews in New York, who were East European Jews and spoke Yiddish. I didn't know any Yiddish.

TD: You are talking about the "bad-manners" passage in *Fragments of an Analysis with Freud*?[1]

JW: Yes. I was taunting Freud about this Jewishness. He himself, of course, was an atheist. He said the segregation of the Jews was not a matter of choice. Of course, Vienna was a rampant anti-Semitic center from way back, and he was exposed to plenty of that. On the other hand, the middle-class Jewish intellectuals in Vienna for the most part had relatively high positions in the cultural scheme of things. Alfred Adler, Stekel, Schnitzler the novelist, Mahler the composer—there were quite a few distinguished Jewish names in the Viennese culture. And the old Austro-Hungarian Empire practiced as a matter of law and principle a high level of tolerance toward the Jews, who were allowed to flourish—though not without some exposure to anti-Semitism. However, with the breakup of the empire and the impoverishment of Austria, and with all the competitive rivalries, there was a revival of anti-Semitism in the period when I was there—and also fascism was emerging.

So it was a very threatening period for Jews, and I was interested in sounding Freud out on his position. But, typically, he said to me, and this I guess summarizes his attitude, "I would have had no objection if any of my children had married a Gentile. But they happened to have married Jews because the Gentiles who were available to them didn't meet their standards." He also, and this is rather important and striking, made no apology—no hint of an apology—for being Jewish. And when I taunted him with these anti-Semitic statements, which I didn't fully believe in—I was sort of sounding him out—he said the Jews have nothing to apologize for. When I said they are too intellectual and don't go into sports, he said, "Whenever they had the opportunity to go into sports they have done very well." And he said, "We have a disproportionately high number of Nobel Prize winners, and the intellectual tradition is something to be proud of

1. "'Jews have bad manners,' I said, 'especially in New York'" (Wortis 1985: 145).

and not to be ashamed of." He held his head up as a Jew in a way that most middle-class Jews did not. A number of the middle- to upper-middle-class Jews in Vienna would get themselves baptized and pass themselves off as Christians. But that was not Freud's way. He also celebrated the foundation of Israel. But he never denied his atheism; he was essentially antireligious. So in these respects I think he was quite admirable.

TD: Could you say something about the role of negative transference in your analysis?

JW: People often say, you know, "You had negative transference to Freud." That isn't true at all. As a personality Freud was very interesting and very attractive. Trouble was he was wrong, you see. I say that in science and in politics, the important thing is to be right. That's also the most difficult thing. His formulations, generally speaking, in the social context in which they emerged, were quite advanced. But times move on. The emphasis that he brought into the field of psychiatry, the whole area of interest in psychology, was a progressive achievement. But the same views and theories adhered to over a period become a drag on science. Many of the views of Freud and his followers, particularly in the U.S.A., I regard as essentially reactionary. I don't want to go into detail, but their tendency to view human personality and human psychology out of the social context is very bad.

Now, Freud, if he were here, would say, "Oh, we don't do that at all!" But in psychiatry, as in many complex fields, it's not a question of whether this or that statement is true, it's what you emphasize. And there is an *enormous* emphasis on the subjective, on the past, and an enormous de-emphasis on the reality of the present. And that is why the psychoanalytic orientation is reactionary. Take the field of social work—and my late wife was a social worker. I would call up some social agency and say, I have a problem for you—can you be helpful? It concerns an old lady who lives with her daughter, but has no social life, and has nothing to do. They say yes, we'll be glad to accept this "client," as they say, and the daughter goes there. Immediately the social worker, who is indoctrinated by psychoanalysis, begins to probe the young lady: "Why are you so guilt-ridden about your mother? What about your relationship with your mother? What have you done that makes you feel so guilty and so responsible?" And she immediately gets into the whole subjective aspect of the problem, instead of dealing with the realities of the situation. This is typical of the way psychoanalysts view the world—and it's very bad. You multiply that a thousand- or a millionfold and people begin to think that way. I mean, Freud went so far as to think war is a product of the innate aggressiveness of man. How wrong can you be? So I would say this is a great incubus or fault that the psychoanalytic orientation shares with many other psychotherapeutic approaches. It is a very harmful thing in our society.

TD: In the analytic setting, it seems the patient must enter into Freud's own discourse, his unconscious, which in turn makes the "cure" possible.

JW: Well, obviously. Freud said that explicitly. He was quite dogmatic, and did not like disagreement. "Analysis is not a relationship between equals," he said. "You are a student, and I'm your teacher." When I would protest about something—his interpretations—he used the Viennese dialect term, saying, "You know a *Schmarn* about psychoanalysis." It's hard to translate the word *Schmarn*, but a vulgar translation would be, "You know shit about analysis." He said, "You don't have the right to query my interpretation."

TD: He said a very similar thing to Ernest Jones once. He said something like, "You should accept psychoanalysis first, and then criticize." But once you accept the discourse of psychoanalysis—

JW: It's a catch-22. You can't understand analysis unless you're analyzed yourself. And you can't go through an analysis unless you give up your resistance. So, you know, it's like Catholicism: you have to be indoctrinated and then accept the dictates of the Pope, otherwise you are an outsider looking in. The whole hierarchical structure of the psychoanalytic movement, requiring every adherent to be himself analyzed, ensures to a high degree—although there are many rebels and dissidents—the maintenance of the theoretical beliefs.

TD: And the transference onto Freud.

JW: Well, we never got much into transference. From Freud's point of view my analysis was very incomplete. He agreed to the four-month arrangement in advance. He said, "Since you're a student we can allow an exception." Actually, when I came back to this country, my intent was to continue my analysis. I was in touch with A. A. Brill and began to look around. But I brought back news of the sensational insulin shock treatment—which was quite a successful treatment for schizophrenia. That aroused big excitement and I was put in charge of the insulin treatment service at Bellevue Hospital. It thrust me into the limelight, with a lot of publicity and attention, and served to make me independent of the need to become an analyst. So I allowed myself to be more skeptical and more resistant, and I decided, "Look, I don't believe in the thing, why should I go through with it?" From a careerist point of view, I lost a golden opportunity to become an analyst, a pupil of Freud, and so forth. But I don't regret that decision. In that period, you know, I was a young man and wasn't that sure of myself, in spite of the fact that in my book I contested a lot of things that Freud said. But you're supposed to be honest in an analysis. If he said that a dream of people lined up entering a house represented children leaving the womb, I would say that's nonsensical—or so it seemed to me [chuckling].

TD: Your analysis comes off as a failure.

JW: Although Freud wrote to me that "it was no immediate success," he didn't regard it as a failure. He said, "The resumption of your relationship to Schilder"—Paul Schilder was an analyst from Vienna with whom I worked—"gives assurance that you will never underestimate the psychological factors in psychiatry." I don't think he would have said it was a failure.

TD: But perhaps he was looking for a new adherent in New York and was trying to keep you within the fold.

JW: I don't think there was any stratagem involved. He just spoke his mind. In my relation with him he was never in any way devious in how he worked. About his handling of the psychoanalytic movement, I don't know. Did you see the 1993 article by Frederick Crews in *The New York Review of Books*? Crews has been a correspondent with me and was very enthusiastic about my book. But I didn't like his article because he demonizes Freud instead of dealing substantively with the scientific issues that Freudianism raises. So from that point of view, although it was anti-Freudian, I didn't like it. Well, he's a literary figure, not a scientist.

TD: Do you think you would have become an analyst if it wasn't for the new shock treatment?

JW: Things are much simpler than that. I would have been an analyst if it had convinced me that it was sound, scientific, and correct.

TD: Beyond the economic advantages of becoming an analyst in New York City?

JW: Economics didn't occur to me. I was a fortunate recipient of a fellowship, so I was very well situated. It was supposed to be a lifetime fellow-ship, but it terminated in seven years since I could not honestly go along with the hopes and wishes of the family of A. Kingsley Porter, a distin-guished Harvard professor. Porter was a homosexual, in the closet, who in the 1930s could not afford to come out with his homosexuality. He fell in love with a young man, whom I knew, Alan Campbell, and the young man spurned him and [Porter] went into a deep depression. He had a summer home in Ireland and he threw himself off the cliffs; his body was never recovered. The bereaved widow, Mrs. Porter, went to Havelock Ellis, who was a friend of Kingsley Porter, saying she wanted to use her wealth to do something for the cause of homosexuality. Ellis, with whom I was in touch at this time, suggested that the best investment would be in a person, not an institution. In turn, he proposed me and I received this fellowship. I was supposed to devote myself to the cause of homosexuality. Well, first of all, I had no wish to be a sexologist. For me that game had been played out by Havelock Ellis and others; sex at that point was being overrated as an object of interest. But I agreed to a compromise arrangement that would allow me to get my psychiatric training, after which time I would devote myself to sex research.

I did get my training, but then, interestingly—and I guess charac-teristically—I reached opinions of my own about the nature of homosex-uality. I got the idea from J. B. S. Haldane, the great physiologist at the University of London, who was very nice to me. Haldane, a great man, said to me, "The trouble with sex research is that most people think it's an unconditioned reflex, but it's really a conditioned reflex." Well, that touched something in me. I began to look at patient material I saw in terms of conditioning, early training, and sure enough, in most cases—not in all, sometimes it's very obscure—you can see the early indoctrination and training.

These views were quite at variance with the views of the widow of this man, who thought her poor husband was born this way, couldn't help it, that his rights needed to be defended, and that science should come to the defense. Since by that time I was immersed in the new approaches to psychiatry, we sort of agreed to part ways. That's why I terminated after seven years; again, a matter of my views.

TD: Was your first introduction to psychoanalysis through Schilder at Bellevue?

JW: Well, if you understand a little about how medical training works, that would not be the way to ask the question. I served a residency at Bellevue Hospital and was on the house staff there. It was kind of an unstructured situation. This new building had to be filled with unpaid staff, so I was the first unpaid—they had formerly called them "alienists"—doctor on the staff. Schilder was one of the senior physicians and I sort of attached myself to him. I used to go around with him while he did rounds, but there was no suggestion of anything like analytic training at all. I was just exposed to some of his thinking. He was somewhat unorthodox. He himself had never been analyzed, but was kind of respected by Freud. He was known around the hospital because he had already achieved some distinction in Vienna. Actually, he had quite an inconspicuous position on the staff at the Bellevue. He was given the title of professor, but had no real assignment. He would float around and make brilliant observations, make a lot of speeches, write a lot of books, but he was not accepted into the old-boy network of American psychiatry.

TD: One of the most interesting aspects of your book is the account of Freud's technical unorthodoxy—which was read, I think, with disbelief in the 1950s.

JW: Freud himself explained that. I would ask him if it was all right to read some of his books during the discussions, and he would say, "Well, since you're a student, it's all right." He would have thrown me out because he got impatient with me, but he didn't want to acknowledge his failure. Also I came under the grand auspices of Havelock Ellis and Adolph Meyer, who was the leading American psychiatrist at that time and one of my mentors. So he had to put up with me.

Some people have questioned this whole business of my keeping notes. But I honestly had no intention whatsoever—considering the personal nature of the material—of publishing these notes. Since I knew it was going to be a limited time, I wanted to preserve a record for later, more deliberate, consideration. People in Vienna in those days spent a lot of time in coffeehouses [*chuckle*]; the waiters expected you to sit there for hours and you were never thrown out. So I would go to my regular cafe—Cafe Astoria—after the sessions, and I would pull out these four-by-six cards and write notes about what happened. It was only twenty years later that I saw them in my file and thought, "What the hell am I going to do with them?" By that time they didn't seem very personal and I thought,

"Look, they're going to be published sometime; why should they be published posthumously? I might as well have the fun of publishing them in my lifetime." So I decided to publish them. But that was an afterthought.

TD: In both the 1940 essay about your analysis and in the book of 1954, you use the word *fragments.*

JW: I used the word *fragments* because it was incomplete. It was not selective in the sense that I omitted anything; maybe two or three references that would have been an embarrassment to me or someone else. So it was an honest account . . .

TD: The book is taken completely from your notes?

JW: Yes, they are pretty much as published. Practically identical. I gave it to my secretary to type up and that was submitted as the manuscript.

TD: I thought you might have been encouraged to publish the full account in 1954 because of the Jones biography in 1953.

JW: That had nothing to do with it; I didn't even know about Jones's biography. I might have one of the Jones volumes, but I don't think I ever read his biography through.

TD: And he doesn't cite your book at all in the following volumes.

JW: Well, with Peter Gay, it's an even worse offense. Gay communicated with me, wrote to me, wanted information, and so on, and then he wrote his big book, *Freud: A Life for Our Time* [1988]. My book, one of the very few accounts of an analysis with Freud, isn't even mentioned. Well, that's biased, I think. He's a dyed-in-the-wool analyst and didn't want to call attention to a work that would be less than reverential to Freud. The fact that he corresponded with me and knew all about me, sent me flattering letters, and then omitted any reference to me shows that he's a person that can't be relied upon. As a matter of fact, he got into trouble over another piece he wrote [for *Harper's*]. He wrote a piece that was represented as a contemporary review of one of Freud's early works. But he gave no hint that this was pure fiction. He only subsequently said, when he was called to order, that he did it as a spoof. So he's a devious character.

I'm now reading a book called *The Great White Lie,* written by a former drug agent, that exposes the devious dealings of our government in handling the drug traffic. It shows the shocking dishonesty of our government that, on the one hand, had its authorities support with money good, reliable, anticommunist and fascist elements in Central America and, on the other hand, had another agency of government arrest these guys for drug smuggling. And they would be released under orders from the CIA [Central Intelligence Agency] because they were good anticommunists—like Noriega at first. This deviousness, which occurs in this grand scale involving the deaths of countless people and the disestablishment or destabilization of governments, happens on an awful scale in government. But it goes on in science too. Or at least in some sections of science, where people fight tooth and nail to defend their views and their interests. You have a character like Gay omitting evidence that doesn't fit in with his scheme; this kind of game goes on, unfortunately. People of real integrity are unfortunately not the most common pattern. Talking about the dissidents who rebelled against him, Freud said to me, "The trouble is not the rights and wrongs of these issues. The trouble is that people just lack character."

TD: It's a recurrent theme with Freud to say that people are in general unworthy.

JW: He was kind of pessimistic in his view of human nature. I once spoke, for example, about the sexologist, Magnus Hirschfeld, and Freud called him an obnoxious rascal.

TD: And he listed off his perversions, didn't he?

JW: Yes. He would say in a kind of hushed voice, "You know, he's homosexual." And I would say, "So what?" He said, "He's not only homosexual, but he had the strangest perversions" [*chuckles*]. The readers whom I appreciate most regard my book as humorous, and in this spirit I said to Freud, "Who knows what high-minded thoughts they have in the course of the act" [*chuckling*]. He said, "Never mind about high-minded thoughts; even in normal sex you don't have high-minded thoughts."

TD: Freud also made a few remarks about Wilhelm Stekel.

JW: Well, I once met Stekel on the street. You see, Vienna is a relatively small city. I said, "How do you do, Dr. Stekel? I'm on my way to my hour with Freud." He said, "Oh, you can learn a great deal from Freud. I require all my pupils to read his works," et cetera. After we chat a little, I come up to Freud, lay on the couch, and say, "Herr Professor, I just met Stekel and he spoke very highly of you, said his pupils are required to read your works and that I can learn a great deal from you." And Freud said, "Very nice of Stekel. He's always ready to forgive me for the things he did to me" [*laughing*]. Typical Freud statement; he always had a sharp tongue.

TD: In "Envois, 1984," appended to the new edition [1985] of your book, you say something to the effect that the future of psychoanalysis lies in an appreciation or recognition of it as a *historical* movement.

JW: I don't quite say that. You use the word *appreciation*, which implies that it had a great positive contribution, but I regard its influence as essentially negative in the culture. Essentially—that doesn't mean that there aren't good elements in it. So yes, I can concede that psychoanalysis made this or that contribution. But the overall impact on the culture today is negative, so I wouldn't "appreciate" it. I would say it's very interesting to raise a question of why the psychoanalytic movement wielded such an enormous influence on the culture of our time. Why did it? *That* poses an interesting question. I give some suggestions as to why I think that happened in *Fragments*.

As a Marxist, I see the Western world as in the agony or death throes of capitalism. I say agony or death throes because I don't think capitalism is working. I have homeless people on my doorstep sometimes! Drug addiction, crime, the disintegration of personality, the alienation, the racism. I see so many evidences of social breakdown and decline that I cannot regard capitalism, at this stage, as viable. I mean, at earlier stages, capitalism was a progressive force—the promotion of individualism, private enterprise— that led to the growth of industry. But many things in history that at one stage represent an advance later become a drag. Capitalism as an economic system is not working. But we're all exposed to the propaganda that favors capitalism. President Clinton and most others equate the free market with democracy. They don't like to use the word *capitalism*; democracy and the free market they regard as synonymous. Well I, of course, don't regard them as synonymous. I regard them as actually contrary and incompatible with each other. Because unless democracy includes economic democracy, it's not real democracy; the same people who control the media control the elections and control the elected officials. It costs four million dollars to run for senator in the United States! So capitalism is incompatible with democracy. We're exposed to propaganda from the cradle to the grave, highlighting individualism. Everyone is a law unto himself, within certain limits. And any red-blooded American can make it big.

Well, psychoanalysis emphasizes individualism. Everything comes from within you: how you behave is a result of your past, your instinctive drives, and so on. So there's an enormous confluence and identity of interests with capitalist ideology and subjective idealism in psychoanalysis.

It enormously emphasizes the subjective and plays down the social. Well, that's very compatible with capitalist ideology, and I think that explains the enormous attraction and popularity of psychoanalysis.

TD: You mentioned before we began that you were at one time a communist.

JW: Yes, I was a member of the Communist Party, but not for a very long period. When I returned from the six or seven years I spent in Europe, I came back to the States in the midst of the Great Depression. All my friends were, I'd say, left wing; some of them were members of the Communist Party, some of them sympathizers. But none of my friends were satisfied with the way things were. My wife, who was a wonderful person, was involved in changing the social order. So I went along with it. That was in the 1930s.

TD: She was an activist?

JW: She was a member of the party, which in those days meant that you attended meetings. It was relatively open, because the Roosevelt period was not as rabidly anticommunistic as was the subsequent period. Roosevelt himself, who was the greatest president of [the twentieth] century, was a capitalist, but a very liberal one. Beleaguered, he welcomed support from all sources, including the left-wing elements. So it was a period of relative acceptance of communism. But at any rate, many of us became advocates of change in the social system with the hope that socialism provided a more rational goal for our economic organization. I joined the Communist Party. Being a member meant meeting from time to time to discuss lines of action. It didn't lead to a life very different from what the well-meaning liberal would have led. I was from very early on an advocate of national health insurance, which is the system you have in Canada.

So my communism did not mean anything special in those days. Then I entered the uniformed services during the war. I became an officer in the Public Health Service, assigned to the navy, and I wore a naval uniform. I dropped out of politics probably in the early 1940s and never returned to the Communist Party. But I still subscribe to left-wing journals. I still embrace, essentially, the Marxist ideology, which permeates my thinking on social relationships constantly. My thinking has been pretty consistent over the years—my socially minded approach, or Marxist approach. I use the terms synonymously.

TD: You were also a member of the American-Soviet Medical Society.

JW: Yes, that was a special thing that arose. Do you know my book, *Soviet Psychiatry* [1950]? During the war we were allies with the Soviet Union and there was a great interest in what they were doing in science. Many scientists in all fields wanted to catch up with Soviet developments. I was never, because of the international situation, allowed to visit the Soviet Union. I got an American visa to go there but the Soviets wouldn't let me in. So it ended up as a compilation of the literature. It was only ten years after it appeared that I made my first visit. After the book appeared I got a grant from the National Institute of Mental Health to continue my reports on Soviet psychiatry. So I had a long involvement. I made four or five visits to the Soviet Union subsequent to this, and have many contacts there.

TD: Were you a victim of McCarthyism?

JW: Oh, yes. I was promptly called before a congressional committee, where they tried to smear me.

TD: Did it succeed?

JW: It hampered my career to some extent, but I seem to have weathered through all of it. I now have a good standing in my profession. People kind of respect me these days for having been hailed before a congressional committee.

TD: And for persevering?

JW: Well, they respect me because of what they regard as my principles, which I did not abandon. But the congressional committee was only interested in self-serving publicity. I went to the Senate house to look up the minutes, and these scoundrels doctored the actual minutes of the meeting! I mean, they're just utterly irresponsible.

According to the American Constitution, a witness in a criminal or potentially criminal investigation cannot be required to testify against himself—that's the Fifth Amendment of the Constitution. And a lot of people got called before McCarthy in those days and pleaded the Fifth when they were asked if they were members of the Communist Party. Of course, that was regarded as tantamount to a confession of guilt. Well, I wouldn't plead the Fifth [*chuckle*]. When asked, I said I was not a member of the Communist Party at the time I wrote *Soviet Psychiatry*. Which is true. As I said, I had given up my membership. But I wouldn't tell them anything more, and they asked if I would plead the Fifth. I said, "No! I do not wish to be a party to *your* attempt to subvert the system." Well, some of those phrases were changed to make me look a little more guilty. Not that anybody reads those things buried in the archives. A couple other things were altered. I could see the alterations in the record; they were written in hand over the typed script.

TD: Apparently, psychoanalysis is on the upswing in Russia.

JW: Well, all the cults are on the upswing now. In Russia, people are reaching back to religion, mysticism, superstition, and, among other things, psychoanalysis is experiencing a certain revival. But they don't have the money for psychoanalysis. For psychoanalysis to flourish you need a big, neurotic middle class able to pay for psychotherapy.

TD: Or you live wherever it's still covered by health insurance.

JW: Yes. In Germany they pay for, I don't know, perhaps three hundred hours of psychoanalysis. In Latin America the only country that meets the requirement of having a big, neurotic middle class is Argentina. You take a country like India and psychoanalysis is practically nonexistent; nobody can afford it.

TD: One of the first things that struck me about your book is the word *didactic* analysis.

JW: Well, that makes no difference in the conduct of an analysis; there's just a difference in the purpose of the analysis. A therapeutic analysis is supposed to relieve a psychiatric or personality or neurotic problem. A didactic analysis is supposed to be a teaching experience. Psychoanalysts assume that practically everybody is more or less neurotic, so Freud flattered me by saying I was more or less normal [*chuckle*]. But he didn't let me go scot-free.

TD: But most analysts would take issue with the idea that you had a didactic analysis, since a didactic analysis is reserved for those who are training to become analysts. The new foreword [1985] to your *Fragments* by Robert Michels argues that your experience wasn't even an analysis—let alone a didactic one.

JW: Michels, a friend of mine, didn't want to give the book his full endorsement because he's a psychoanalyst himself. I mean, psychoanalysis is like religion. I can have all kinds of political differences with acquaintances, but you raise a question about the efficacy or validity of psychoanalysis to somebody who has invested three years of his life and, having been analyzed, has made a profession out of being an analyst, or on the basis of his analytic insights has changed his wife and done God knows what—you question him a little bit and you open a storm of opposition.

I've seen people argue until they are blue in the face about psychoanalysis. So it touches people's sensibilities.

TD: Just a moment ago you said "changed his wife" instead of "changed his life."

JW: No, I *meant* "change his wife"! People go through analysis and they get insights that supposedly explain why they're not getting along with their wife. For example, their wife evokes bad memories of their relationship with their mother—and that explains the incompatibility. God knows, people with these cockeyed insights change their lives or their wives. You come along and say this procedure is invalid and they'll fight tooth and nail.

TD: What did you think of Phyllis Grosskurth's 1980 biography of Ellis?

JW: She's a good friend of mine, but I didn't like her book about Ellis. She is deeply immersed in Freudian ways of thinking, and has the mistaken notion that the key to understanding Havelock Ellis's life was the fact that he was sexually impotent—which I don't think was true.

TD: You don't think it's true that he was impotent?

JW: Well, he was and he wasn't. He was very shy, had a kind of puritanical upbringing, and, like Shaw, didn't have a sexual experience till he was close to 30. He probably was no Don Juan. His wife turned out, after the marriage, to be homosexual—or she became homosexual afterwards. Nevertheless, he had a real love relationship with his wife and a really intense passion. Being the kind of person he was, he tolerated her homosexual attachment to another woman. They lived separately by design—so I don't think he had much of a conventional sex life. He also was fascinated by urination, which again goes back to a childhood experience: he was walking on a country lane with his mother, when she left him on the road and raised her skirt and urinated. He was most impressed by that [*chuckle*]. He was always fascinated by urination—which I regard as a harmless interest. But Pat Grosskurth makes much of that. Ellis had a number of intimate relationships with women; how far they went I don't know. After the death of his wife, he had a very close and committed relationship with Françoise Lafitte, whom I knew—a French woman who was entangled in legalities such that she could never marry him. But I knew her and her two boys, and *she* certainly was not impotent.

I would say that he had a rather shy and inhibited sexuality, but to build his whole lifework around it is a mistake. Grosskurth told me once in London that "I don't like Havelock Ellis." That's not a good credential for writing about Ellis. Also, she's a literary figure, not a scientist. In general, I think she undervalues Ellis and has contributed to the disparagement of Ellis by writing that kind of biography. She has no real appreciation for him.

TD: Yes, but she brings up the question of your adulation for him.

JW: Well, that's what happens in biography. The few references she has to me are about 50 percent wrong.

TD: Is that right?

JW: Yes. She said that I resisted Freud because I was being loyal to Ellis—which is absurd; it never crossed my mind. I objected to Freud when he said things that were *wrong*; it had nothing to do with Ellis. See, that's the psychoanalytic interpretation. She also refers to a French poem which was kind of offensive.

TD: Yes, by Wladimir Granoff.

JW: "Why does this man sit in judgment of Freud? Well, the reason is because he has an ass."[2] That's ludicrous. I mean it's stupid. Actually Pat and I have had a very good relationship. But, you know, we have differences of opinion.

TD: Hilda Doolittle also wrote an account of her analysis with Freud.

JW: She became very close friends with Freud. I think they had kind of an affectionate relationship. Part of the book she wrote, called *Tribute to Freud* [1974], is what I would call a dithyrambic account of her relation to Freud. She regarded him as a kind of godlike figure. It's quite different from the way I recorded my experience [*chuckle*]. She also happened to be a friend of Ellis's. She was in Vienna when I was there and Ellis told me to look her up, but I didn't. I didn't bother, although Freud said to me, "You should. She's an interesting person." I said, "I'm too shy to talk to total strangers for no reason at all." He said, "That's all right; it's natural for young people to be shy. You shouldn't worry about that. Until you find your place in the world, most people *should* be shy." He was very human in all of these things.

2. The lines from Granoff, inspired by Pushkin, are: "A l'Académie des sciences / Siège le prince Outrance. / Pourquoi a-t-il ce siège? / Pourquoi ce grand honneur? / C'est très simple, il a ce siege / Parce qu'il a un postérieur."

TD: How did the analysis affect your weekends, your time with your wife?

JW: It was just an hour a day. We went merrily about our business. I'd come home to my wife and say, "He gave me a rough time today." She'd say, "Let's go out and have a goulash" [*laughter*].

TD: Freud at one point told you to tell your wife to stay out of the analysis; she had said that maybe you were being too sensitive. It was typical of Freud to get involved—

JW: He used the word *leak*. He said there shouldn't be any leaks in the analysis; in other words, I shouldn't be discussing this with somebody else, because that means you will abreact, digest the experience, with someone else. Someone who doesn't have the right to sit in on your experience.

TD: In closing, could you say something about the reception of *Fragments*? There was, for instance, the parody written in the *New Yorker* in 1955—which I found quite amusing.

JW: Well, since I was the butt of the humor—

TD: I thought the whole situation was parodied: the dogs—

JW: Well, humor has a context and value system. The whole point of the joke is this: imagine the patient analyzing Freud, the absurdity of it. Well, that presupposes a sort of adulatory attitude towards Freud. To me it doesn't seem absurd for a patient, who is critical, to evaluate scientifically the methods of an analyst. It doesn't seem absurd or presumptuous; to me the element of absurdity is missing. Therefore I don't laugh at it.

Fragments got mixed reviews, but was mostly neglected. Interestingly, left-wing journals didn't like it. Why? Because the left-wing movement in those days was all immersed in psychoanalysis. It's hard to say the emperor has no clothes when everybody thinks he has clothes on. It was very hard to resist at a time when our educated middle classes were all gung ho for psychoanalysis. It was very hard to assume a critical posture. But now things have changed. Psychoanalysts are more on the defensive these days.

2

An American Woman in Freud's Vienna:
Esther Menaker on Freudianism and Her Analysis
with Anna Freud

Interviewed by Todd Dufresne

Esther Menaker attended the University of Pennsylvania, where she studied science and, later, psychology. After that, she received psychoanalytic training in Vienna in the 1930s. During this rich period, Esther and her husband, William, also received PhDs in clinical psychology from the University of Vienna. Menaker was on the faculty of the New York University Postdoctoral Program in Psychoanalysis and Psychotherapy. She died in August 2003.

Her books include *Masochism and the Emergent Ego* (1979), *Separation, Will, and Creativity* (1984), and *Appointment in Vienna* (1989). *Appointment in Vienna* is one of a short list of books written by someone intimate with Freud's Vienna. During the 1930s, Esther and William had arranged for analyses with Anna Freud and Helene Deutsch, respectively. The couple stayed in Vienna for a total of five years, giving Esther plenty of opportunity to see the psychoanalytic culture up close.

Menaker spoke candidly about psychoanalysis during our conversation, which took place in her apartment in Manhattan on October 13, 1997. She was 90 years old. At one point she admits to having long "outgrown psychoanalysis," preferring instead the self psychology of Heinz Kohut and the will psychology of Otto Rank (see Menaker, 1984). Menaker was an authority on Rank, having written two books on his work (Menaker 1982, 1996). She was also a pioneer of the theory of masochism. Although some consider these works classics in the field, Menaker mentioned at the outset how forgetful the psychoanalytic literature can be. This interview might help stem the tide in that regard.

. . .

TD: What role did sexuality play in your analysis with Anna Freud in 1930?

EM: I grew up in America in the 1920s, during the flapper era, when people were more liberal, sexually speaking, than their Viennese counterparts. So basically I found the atmosphere of Vienna very conservative, if not reactionary. During my very first analytic session, I dutifully told Anna Freud of my sexual adventures—but only with great difficulty. Remember, I was young, not quite liberated, and Anna Freud was a stranger to me. After I recounted my exploits, I stood up from the couch and told her how exhausted I was from the effort. Anna, in turn, said that there was nothing unusual about my stories, adding that she had often heard of such things. Now, she said this in a very disparaging way, as if to say I should not be so proud of my progressiveness. I felt she was angling for my narcissism. That, in any case, was the tone and atmosphere of psychoanalysis in Vienna: to put you down, and never encourage or affirm the self. And that is why I became attracted to the works of Otto Rank and Heinz Kohut.

TD: Was your attraction to psychoanalysis motivated by youthful rebellion?

EM: I did not choose psychoanalysis, nor was I particularly "attracted" to it. Really, I became interested through the influence of my husband, who became interested in psychoanalysis after an unfulfilling career as a dentist. When Bill and I met we were both involved in the social-work world, which provided a natural bridge to psychology. My background was, however, in the sciences. I studied chemistry at college, and my father was a working scientist. For this reason my interest in psychoanalysis was scientific. True, I also thought that analytic treatment would be helpful for me personally—something that concerned Anna. The Viennese were suspicious of Americans seeking professional training only.

TD: Despite the conservatism of certain segments of Vienna, I wonder if analysis challenged or even loosened the values of some analysts.

EM: That's an interesting thought. Much to my surprise, there was a lot of infidelity in the psychoanalytic movement. The first rumor that I heard in Vienna was that Dora Hartmann, the wife of Heinz Hartmann, was sleeping with Felix Deutsch. Of course, I don't know if it was true or not.

TD: Was it a culture of gossip?

EM: Yes, a culture of gossip and political conservatism. For example, there was an election in Vienna not long after I arrived, and a little parade passed by the window during a session. Anna asked if I wanted to see the parade at the window, which we did together. I asked her about the meaning of it all, and at one point she said, "Oh, nothing ever changes." I have never forgotten that remark, which is very significant, because of course the philosophy of psychoanalysis dictates that nothing ever changes; we only put the pieces in different places.

In this respect, I think that psychoanalysis is much too invested in resignation. I can do without it. As a friend once said to me, "Esther, you don't have *enough* resignation." Well, that kind of thinking makes me furious [*laughing*].

TD: This advocacy of resignation seems tied up with anti-Americanism, the stereotypical American being optimistic and wealthy. The Viennese resented such optimism, but needed American dollars to float the business of analysis. But, at bottom, they didn't really want you around.

EM: You are absolutely right. You are describing what I felt most of the five years that I lived there. Freud himself hated Americans, which does not endear him to me. Despite the faults of America, it is nonetheless a very great democracy.

TD: So you didn't feel welcome by the analysts?

EM: Not at all. In fact, in my second analysis with Willi Hoffer, I remember one session wherein he claimed that Americans were inconsiderate, sloppy, and so on. To make this point he described a classroom in which a group of Americans met with August Aichhorn for a seminar. Willi said he felt sorry for the children because the Americans had put their cigarette butts into their inkwells. But, you know, there were no ashtrays in the classrooms.

TD: I guess everyone smoked in those days, especially the analysts.

EM: Not always. When I began my first session with Anna, she said to me, "I'm going to be knitting or sewing while I listen to you; that is instead of the smoking of the man." That comment rubbed me the wrong way.

TD: So you haven't taken up knitting?

EM: I never took it up as a habit, nor did I take up smoking, although I smoked a bit in Vienna—about five cigarettes a week. But, as a matter of fact, I love knitting, even though my arthritis has gotten in the way in recent years.

TD: Did you ever knit from behind the couch?

EM: It is so long ago since I used the couch, about thirty years, that I can hardly remember. You know, my couch is, for me, a place to take a nap on. I believe that developing a human relationship with a patient is the important thing, and promote this through face-to-face conversations.

TD: Do your analytic colleagues know of your heresy?

EM: Well, no—since I got rid of the colleagues [*laughing*]. I don't see those people anymore. I have very little contact with people that you would call analysts.

TD: So you wouldn't consider yourself an analyst?

EM: Today I consider myself a psychotherapist. I could do analysis, but don't.

TD: If someone asked you for an analysis, would you?

EM: I think not. Not in the classical sense.

TD: For technical or moral reasons?

EM: Although I have never thought of it that way, I guess my reservations are essentially based on moral considerations. I really do not believe in the practice of psychoanalysis, which is destructive. Psychoanalysis denigrates the individual's self by putting him or her in a submissive, narcissistic position. So I don't think it is good. At best it is suited to those few people who live a submissive life—and which psychoanalysis is only too happy to reinforce. You know, psychoanalysts don't know anything about the art of living. Instead, they teach us to suspect everything, since everything is something other than it seems. It is all very bad. To begin with, it breeds a terrible kind of paranoia.

TD: One of the themes of *Appointment in Vienna* is that reality is constantly undermined by psychoanalytic treatment. Did your turn away from psychoanalysis amount to a return to your early interest in social work?

EM: I was merely a novice in social work, working in a child placement agency. My first job was home-finding, evaluating people who had applied for foster children, which was followed by work with children themselves. That entire time lasted only two years, and then I left for Vienna. Just the same, your remark is quite accurate. I once had a terrible argument with the head of the school of social work, Kenneth Prey, because I thought the tenor of the school was far too psychological and insufficiently focused on social and economic factors. In addition, although I did not grow up with religion, which was considered the opiate of the masses, I grew up a socialist. My parents were Russian revolutionaries.

TD: So was your interest in psychology a mistake?

EM: No, because I also have a deep interest in the inner life. I just don't think that psychoanalysis explains the whole inner life. I have come back, over the last fifteen or twenty years, to very deep personal problems that are religious and spiritual in nature. This extremely important side of life is being lost in the modern world, although there are signs that others share my interest, just as there are signs of a reawakening of spirituality. But the majority of people are committed to the material world.

TD: There certainly is a resurgence of New Age spiritualism and of cults of many varieties. The rise of psychoanalysis may have played a role in all of this, being a secular turn away from religion that is nonetheless its own religion and Weltanschauung.

EM: It was indeed a kind of church, although it is now fallen into some disrepute. In its structure you have to believe in the father, son, and the holy ghost—Freud being all three [*laughing*].

TD: Were you skeptical as a young person learning psychoanalysis, or has this skepticism been read back into this early experience?

EM: There was skepticism from the start. I always had a tendency to ask questions when I read Freud's work—placing question marks in the margin, and so on. I was by no means sure of his claims. But I have always been a skeptic. My parents were involved with social and political questions, and I was very skeptical about this interest as well. I always felt that there is something more to life than that perspective. And I was always skeptical about my mother's attitude toward sexuality. So I would say that I grew up with skepticism, which is part and parcel of my scientific background.

TD: Perhaps your interest in psychoanalysis was a reaction to your parents' socialist background.

EM: Yes, I think you are right. You have to know my college education. I was trained in the hard sciences at the University of Pennsylvania, which at that time only admitted women to the school of education. I therefore had to take as many courses at the college, the male part of the school, as in the other part. In my organic chemistry class I was one woman among eighty men in the lab. The male students were not in any way prejudiced, although we did not discuss it. But I didn't feel uncomfortable, probably because my major good relationship in life was with my father, who, as I say, was a scientist.

After the first three years of college I had completed all the requirements for my major. Consequently I had a chance to take electives in philosophy, anthropology, and psychology. That's when I really got interested in psychological issues. I didn't know anything about psychoanalysis at that point, but I was characteristically curious. So it was with curiosity more than commitment or belief that I went to Vienna.

TD: How did you become interested in Freud's one-time close adherent, Otto Rank?

EM: Rank influenced the school of social work. Moreover, Bill was interested in Rank when we were in Vienna. Once, when he was looking through a Rank book, Helene Deutsch made a point of saying that it was a very bad book. Well, since Bill had a very bad time of his analysis with Deutsch, he probably went right out and bought the book! We brought back to America an interest in Rank, which was heresy. Anna Freud knew I was interested, but said nothing—which is, of course, the analyst's privilege.

TD: Did Anna keep quiet during the analysis?

EM: Yes, but not as quiet as some American analysts that I have heard about.

TD: Freud himself was not always very quiet.

EM: Despite his padded door, I used to hear his voice from the waiting room which he shared with Anna.

TD: Did you ever see Freud?

EM: Oh yes. He would come to the door to get his next patient, while I sat in the waiting room. But I also saw him at their summerhouse in the suburbs, during the so-called hot months. Anna Freud held sessions there, using the little terrace on the ground floor as her waiting room. While I waited there Freud would walk about the garden, looking at the potted cactus. Freud loved cactus. He would greet me, but that was the extent of it.

TD: Did he maintain a professional distance?

EM: I wouldn't say that. The general tone was reserved, somewhat distant, but always courteous.

TD: You didn't engage Freud in banter of any kind?

EM: No.

TD: Were you intimidated?

EM: I am not sure I was intimidated, though that is possible. In any case, I was never in awe of the great man. As you know, we went to Vienna through the kind offices of Fritz Wittels. When we first arrived in Vienna, Wittels invited us to a cafe. During the conversation, I remember him saying that Freud was a genius. While I didn't say anything, I thought that this was an exaggeration. Freud has had a tremendous influence on society— I think too much—and I agree that his discoveries and thinking should be known and evaluated. But he was no Einstein, who was unmistakably a genius. Einstein has influenced our knowledge of the universe, while Freud's legacy remains contested. Freud may have been a great thinker, but greater than Nietzsche or Kant?

TD: Can only a scientist be a genius?

EM: No, no. Artists and writers are capable of genius. I happen to like Einstein not only for his scientific genius, but for his character. I mean, he was a great humanist and truth seeker. Freud is another story: quite simply, I don't like Freud's character. I know a lot more about Freud's life today, and really cannot admire him as a human being. I don't think he was a bad person, or feel about him the way I do about Helene Deutsch. She was such an unpleasant woman. But in general these people I met in Vienna were not honest—none of them, including, it seems, Freud himself.

TD: You and your husband seem to have been treated with disdain.

EM: They treated most Americans with disdain, but they treated us with special disdain because we were not rich. We went to Vienna with a very small amount of money.

TD: So you weren't even good "Americans"!

EM: No, we were not! We weren't good anything.

TD: You say at one point in *Appointment in Vienna* that psychoanalysis has gotten enough right to justify its modification.

EM: That was very smart of me [*laughing*]! I am aware, however, that orthodox analysts do not call such modifications "analysis." My son Tom, an analyst, has a summerhouse in Maine, not far from Kurt Eissler and his wife. One day they met at some rocks, and Tom told Eissler that he was going to study psychoanalysis at the White Institute in New York. Eissler told him that this was not analysis. Such orthodoxy makes it hard for me to answer your earlier question about whether or not I am still an analyst. In this respect I am in the awkward position that Otto Rank found himself in. Of course, no analyst would consider me an analyst anymore. I meet people once a week, and do a great deal of good work on this basis. Also, I do not rely on free association, but engage in a dialogue. In fact I do not speak any differently with a patient than I am with you right now. So I suppose I should not call myself an analyst anymore.

TD: Were you ever influenced by the work of neo-Freudians like Erich Fromm and Erik Erikson?

EM: I knew Fromm, although not terribly well. He was very kind to us, and saw to the Spanish translation of Bill's and my book, *Ego and Evolution* [1965], when he was in Mexico. And I sent a close friend for treatment to Fromm when he came to this country. However, although I respect Fromm's work and think he's an interesting figure, I am a radically independent soul. So, no, I wasn't influenced by Fromm or, for that matter, by Erikson.

With Erikson we had a cordial, social relationship. We would visit in our homes, but we didn't share ideas or anything like that. I had no inkling he would become the figure he became. In Vienna I felt that he was much too devoted to Anna Freud. I remember one day he came to the little school where we taught in a suburb of Vienna. Erikson had a terrible toothache, and said that he was lucky to have the best dentist in the world, saying, "He is Anna Freud's dentist." That was Erikson's reverent tone.

TD: Did you practice child analysis when you returned to America?

EM: Yes, for three years until my second child was born. And then I went into private practice and, since child patients were hard to find in those days, I began an adult practice.

TD: What do you think of child analysis?

EM: Therapeutic work with children can be very helpful. I remember that Berta Bornstein was a natural with children, but I don't know that Anna Freud was that kind of personality. Anna was more of a teacher with children. I must qualify my remarks, however, and say that I really dislike analytic-inspired child therapy. That is not the sort of practice I am speaking about or would recommend.

TD: You mention the play technique in your book.

EM: Everyone used the play technique, including Anna Freud. Once I came into her office for my session and she had a chest with dolls all along the shelf. She said a little child was coming for a session.

TD: Despite your recognition of idealization in psychoanalysis, including what you call the psychoanalytic mystique, nowhere in *Appointment in Vienna* do you discuss suggestion or hypnosis. You do, however, mention that you felt brainwashed.

EM: In retrospect I can say that there must have been tremendous brainwashing and suggestion. For although I was skeptical, it didn't occur to me in a fundamental way that psychoanalysis wasn't true. As you say, it had the quality of a religion. You can measure my early attitude toward psychoanalysis by an episode that I was thinking about recently. Bill and I brought our two-year-old son, Michael, for a visit to my mother in Philadelphia, where she lived in an apartment on the third floor. On her veranda she had numerous potted plants, one of which Michael tossed over the side of the veranda to the ground. Now, I knew what he was planning, but had decided that I should not inhibit even his hostile act. It was all very self-conscious. Naturally, my mother thought this scene was outrageous, and indeed it was. It was an extreme gesture on my part, which came out of a belief that psychoanalysis was right. So that episode is a small measure of how psychoanalysis infected my everyday thinking about things. Despite our doubts, I'm afraid we still believed.

TD: These sorts of stories persuade me to think of the history of psychoanalysis as a comedy, or better, as a farce. Nowadays I tend to think that psychoanalysis is quite dead, except, perhaps, as a field for historical study.

EM: I agree. And, you know, its death is not a tragedy! I am very grateful to have lived long enough to have left psychoanalysis well behind me.

3

Edward Shorter's Deflections on Medicine, History, and Psychoanalysis

Interviewed by Todd Dufresne

Edward Shorter received his PhD from Harvard University in 1967 and then joined the University of Toronto as a member of the Department of History. In 1991 he became the Jason A. Hannah Professor of the History of Medicine. He is the author of numerous books in the history of medicine, including *From Paralysis to Fatigue: A History of Psychosomatic Illness in the Modern Era* (1992), *From the Mind into the Body: The Cultural Origins of Psychosomatic Symptoms* (1994), and *A History of Psychiatry: From the Era of the Asylum to the Age of Prozac* (1997a). Many of Shorter's books critically assess the impact of psychoanalysis on twentieth-century thought. His most recent books are *A Historical Dictionary of Psychiatry* (2005a) and *Written in the Flesh: A History of Desire* (2005b).

Shorter is well known for his frank, often controversial views about such transient mental illnesses as chronic fatigue syndrome and, at least among those who know him, for his distaste for contemporary theory and the shibboleths of *race*, *class*, and *gender*. His critique of psychoanalysis has only sharpened over the last decade, especially in light of his research in biological psychiatry. He was interviewed in his office at the University of Toronto on June 18, 2001, and updated his remarks in August 2005.

. . .

TD: How fair is it to emphasize the many nonscientific impulses in the history of medicine, such as class and gender?

ES: It's part of the history, so it is certainly not unfair. The history of medicine isn't just the record of scientific accomplishments, each of which is more bold than the last. It is also a tale of the frailty of human knowledge when confronted with the inexorability of disease. Like everyone, physicians are deformed by their own gender, social class, personal histories, and the cultural tradition in which they find themselves. All such considerations deflect them from the path of true science, but are a part of the social history of medicine.

TD: Are you at all interested in recent feminist and poststructuralist theoretical discourses, for example, concerning subject positions?

ES: No, I think it's a waste of time. It gives me the hives.

TD: Freud himself put a lot of stock in subjectivity, and to some extent undermined traditional ideas about objectivity and consciousness, all of which has made him attractive to all sorts of fashionable theorists in recent years. What do you think about the influence Freud has had, and continues to have, on our so-called postmodern culture?

ES: I think the influence of psychoanalysis on postmodern culture has been zilch. Young people today don't have the slightest idea who Freud was or what the original ideas of psychoanalysis represented. A better question would be, I think, what was the influence of psychoanalysis on culture from the 1940s to 1960s? Enormous, is the answer, but postmodernism comes later. As for psychoanalysis helping them to "de-repress"—hey, man, they're de-repressed already.

TD: You have written about the role of naming and rhetoric, and language more generally, in the history of medicine. For example, you discuss institutional name changes, when insane asylums began to be called nervous clinics.

ES: The change was the result of the horrible fear that patients had for anything psychiatric, since that meant to them evidence of degeneration. Parents worried that they wouldn't be able to marry their daughters off if it were known that there was psychiatric illness in the family. Nervous illness, by contrast (which affected the physical nerves of the body and was seen as less inheritable), was much more the result of happenstance. So it was more acceptable to have your problems labeled "nervous" or "neurological" rather than "psychiatric."

TD: As a nominalist of sorts, I am certainly intrigued by your comments.

ES: In the history of homosexuality, for example, there are two positions: the realist and the nominalist. The realist basically says that gay men and women are born homosexual and that it is not the culture that encourages them. The nominalist says, "Baby, until we got a name for it, you ain't it." I believe in the realist position and think the nominalist position has grossly distorted the history of sexuality. I hope you don't find this personally offensive, but I think you are on the wrong train.

TD: No, of course not. But we both are able to recognize the power of words to shape a culture, including our illnesses.

ES: There's always a give-and-take between essentialism and nominalism. Neither claims the ballpark for its own. But I think that social forces and biology have a much greater ability to shape people's behavior than words. I'm interested nowadays in the history of sexuality, where biological drives clearly predominate over social construction [see Shorter 2006b].

So, sure, I'd say that naming things has an enormous subjective value. But in the history of sexuality and also in the area of psychiatric illness, the question, again, is this: does the orientation or illness predate the name? The realist position is that it certainly does. I believe that people had biologically based psychiatric illness long before psychiatrists came along to give them names.

TD: What about the *DSM*, the *Diagnostic and Statistical Manual of Mental Disorders*? How does it happen that we go from a very small manual about recognized mental illnesses to what is now a very thick manual?

ES: Arthur Kleinman once said that 90 percent of the diagnoses on the *DSM-III* don't exist, that they are simply artifacts devised for reasons of insurance. I think that's true! But at the same time I don't disparage the nosological enterprise of trying to differentiate and clearly demarcate distinct psychiatric illnesses. I agree that the DSM series has failed to do this very well and has become like a runaway express train. But the basic impulse is a reasonable one. Just as we subdivide and classify the diseases of the chest, why not do the same for illnesses of the mind and brain? Well, of course we can. But the creators of the DSM have ended up with a wildly inappropriate set of classifications and glued themselves to a method that will almost surely lead them into the desert, namely, the consensus method: bringing a bunch of experts together around the table and encouraging them to compromise. Such compromises might be great for the social dynamics of the group, but as a scientific exercise, the results are garbage.

TD: I can sympathize, up to a point, with the realist perspective concerning biological illness. But isn't the situation much looser when it comes to the kinds of psychosomatic illness that Freud dealt with in his everyday practice?

ES: It is looser, because the role of cultural molding is so heavy. Cultural molding in schizophrenia or major depression isn't that dramatic. But with psychosomatic illness such molding dominates the script, dictating to the patient what is and isn't a legitimate symptom. In turn, the patient's mind sees to it that legitimate symptoms are produced. As the cultural sense of what is legitimate changes, the kinds of symptoms a patient presents change as well. Nobody wants to be told that it's all in their mind.

TD: So you reject nominalism as it concerns biological illness but not psychosomatic illness?

ES: No. Whether you call it neurasthenia, depression, or the lights, the symptoms are basically the same. People are tired all the time, may be weepy, have a sense of dejection about their own accomplishments; this has always existed, no matter what you call it, although today we call it major depression.

TD: You do say explicitly, in *From Paralysis to Fatigue* [1992], that the symptoms change in the different eras.

ES: Right. The same underlying impulse to somatize exists, has doubtless existed through the ages, and is doubtless neurogenic or biologically based. Only the expression of it is determined by cultural molding.

TD: In your work, when you argue that there was a "massive duplicity, a century-long deception about professional views of nervousness" [Shorter 1992], just how intended or conscious was that deception by practitioners? Moreover, what role did Freud and psychoanalysis play in this deception?

ES: Psychoanalysis removed the fig leaf of "nervous" entirely. It scared the pants off people. That's why psychoanalysis had relatively little impact on the great mass of average, somatizing patients. It told them, literally, "Madam, it's all in your head."

As for the terms *nervous* and *nervousness*, they were originally designed for public consumption. These were psychiatrists, and they knew perfectly well what psychiatric illness was. And, to them, disorders of the mind could be divorced from disorders of the nerves. So calling it nervous illness, and themselves nerve doctors, was really public relations, something to make the patients feel better, something to draw them in during a time of highly competitive medicine. Later this distinction between public relations, spin control, and what one actually believes does become effaced a bit—and it becomes effaced when we get to the *DSM-III* and after. By contrast, the vogue for nervousness in the nineteenth century was, I think, more duplicitous, more a matter of spin control.

TD: Does that spin control go on today, although we may not yet be able to see it?

ES: It certainly goes on when doctors tell patients that their problems are a result of an imbalance in their serotonin metabolism or their norepinephrine metabolism, because even though the drugs they are given may affect these neurotransmitters, the real problem almost certainly lies elsewhere—in the chemistry of the brain. Psychiatrists today are still very uncertain about what the real problem might be in biological terms, but they tell patients about imbalances because it is reassuring. Pills can then be prescribed to control serotonin, and the patient goes away happy. But the psychiatrists who paid attention to what they learned in psychopharmacology don't believe that at all.

TD: This reminds me of your discussion of the placebo effect in *Bedside Manners* [1985], where you decry the use of serious drugs as placebos.

ES: There is a very serious placebo effect at work here, which in psychotherapy is called suggestion. Instead of giving sugar pills to patients suffering from chronic pain, they are given drugs that have a powerful pharmacological action. This is seen as the only ethically acceptable way of not lying to the patient. The drug probably won't have much impact on their symptoms, but at least people can believe that this is real medical therapy and not just some blasted sugar pill.

TD: Doctors no longer have the cultural authority to prescribe such placebos.

ES: I think it is an intolerable interference in the doctor-patient relationship for bioethicists, whose background is in philosophy, to wave the red flag about such "lying"—even though there's a good chance it might help the patients.

TD: Do you think that Freud ever cured anyone by psychoanalysis?

ES: Psychoanalysis has the same therapeutic power as any other form of psychotherapy, which is to say, a considerable amount. But it has to do with the closeness of the doctor-patient relationship, not with any of the intellectual content of psychoanalysis. And psychoanalysis is much longer and more expensive than, say, cognitive-behavioral therapy.

TD: Reading your work, I am often struck by the financial details you discuss. For example, in your *History of Psychiatry* [1997a], you speak about how the need for psychiatrists to have private practices led to the expansion of psychoanalysis.

ES: Psychoanalysis became the keystone of private practice, although only about 10 percent of private practitioners engaged in analysis. But psychodynamic doctoring really came to dominate psychotherapeutic approaches in private practice.

TD: How much of a deflection is finance in the history of medicine?

ES: Money was a very powerful incentive to get psychiatrists out of the asylum and into a mainstream practice, where they would rejoin the rest of civil society—and make a lot more. At the same time, patients demanded psychoanalytic treatment. So you could say they were just fulfilling legitimate consumer desire. The analysts, even in their best days, didn't make as much as neurologists or cardiovascular surgeons. So if they chose psychoanalysis it was for other motives than material gain. Economic motivation has a role to play, but it isn't the full story. If you overemphasize economics, you couldn't explain why anyone ever went into psychiatry. Even being a Park Avenue analyst never compared with other specialties on that street.

TD: Except that, surely, many practitioners of psychoanalysis could never have succeeded in those specialties.

ES: But they were all medically qualified. If they didn't go into ophthalmology residency, I don't think it was because they were incompetent or inferior, but because they were attracted to analysis for other reasons.

TD: In *Before Freud* of 1987, Francis Gosling argues something that seems to me counterintuitive, namely, that neurasthenia was not limited to the upper classes in America, but was in fact a regular part of a doctor's working-class clientele.

ES: It's just that many of the physicians that wrote about neurasthenia happen to have had upper-class practices. But it doesn't mean that neurasthenia is limited to the upper classes, any more than it would mean that only the upper class today suffers from depression!

TD: But aren't certain illnesses the privilege of the rich?

ES: Neurasthenia is not a good example, because it is just another word for depression. Take, rather, the sofa cases: women who took to their beds and remained there for years. That was indeed a disease of rich women. Normal women couldn't afford it. Who would run the family? Who would go out and help make a living?

TD: I have always entertained what may be a comforting illusion, namely, that lack of money at least keeps indulgent illness away, that the working class may in some ways be healthier than the upper class.

ES: If anything, the working classes are less hardy, because their health isn't as good as the health of the middle class and because they don't care for themselves as well. But working-class people are just as subject to depression as any other class.

TD: Let me push this a bit more. In *Bedside Manners*, you discuss the transition from the traditional, to the modern, to the postmodern patient. You seem to imply that working-class patients have neither the time nor the desire for self-reflection, which is more characteristic of the middle classes. You don't see a connection between this heightened capacity for introspection and, say, the rise of the postmodern patient?

ES: I'm not sure if this is an argument I would want to pursue very far, but, clearly, patients who develop lots of insight are sometimes able to shed psychosomatic symptoms. That is, there is an inverse relation between insight and somaticizing. At the same time, as a real proposition, almost no one with a major psychosomatic illness, regardless of social class, has any insight at all. They all believe that it is totally organic.

TD: Do you think psychoanalysis promotes insight?

ES: I think that its vouchsafes are valueless as such, because they rest on a bankrupt intellectual base. Astrology promotes insight as well, but those are equally valueless. Are you better because you have the insight that your relationship to the maternal breast was X rather than Y? Gimme a break.

TD: How did Freud manage to escape the appearance of malpractice, given, in retrospect, the clear indications of suggestion in his practice?

ES: Good question. Why hasn't psychoanalysis today been the object of massive class action lawsuits on behalf of all the patients mistreated by analysts for conditions that we now recognize to be amenable to pharmacotherapy? Or those illnesses, at least, that we know were not psychogenic? For example, Tourette's syndrome: for many years these patients were treated by psychoanalysis, the most inappropriate treatment possible. Even today it's a mystery to me why the Tourette's patients of analysis haven't banded together to sue the American Psychoanalytic Association, or individual analysts, for all the mischief they did.

It's a similar situation with Freud, as you say. Why wasn't he sued? First of all, because nobody got sued for malpractice in those days. The concept was scarcely visible on anyone's radar. Second, because a lot of people believed in this stuff—especially in the middle classes—right up to the 1970s, and on both sides of the ocean. So, naturally, a malpractice suit would have been thrown out by a middle-class judge or middle-class jury. They all believed in the doctrine of psychogenicity based on unconscious conflicts, and so by initiating legal action you would have been a laughing-stock and wasted your money as well.

TD: What about trained academics?

ES: Well, the academic establishment did call him on it and never did stomach psychoanalysis. They remained much more biologically oriented, and didn't believe at all in infantile sexuality. But academic psychiatry is quite different from community psychiatry. In community psychiatry you have to make your money based on what people will pay you. If patients start to believe this stuff, then you better do it—or you won't have any patients.

TD: Given that somatizing is a regular part of everyday life, what does it mean to speak of simulated or even faked illness?

ES: There is a spectrum of self-insight. People who have 100 percent self-insight and still somatize are really faking it. People who have zero insight and somatize have a major psychiatric problem. In other words, there is a smooth continuum that goes from malingering to hysteria, and where you are on that continuum depends on the amount of self-insight you have.

TD: Did Bertha Pappenheim, Breuer's Anna O. and the founding case of psychoanalysis, have any insight into her illness?

ES: Nobody knows. She grew up and became an apparently fully normal social worker. Her basic problem as an adolescent was drug addiction, which she seems later to have ditched. It doesn't require much psychoanalytic insight to grow out of a morphine addiction.

TD: I am curious about your statement, in *From the Mind into the*

Body [1994], that the explanation of suggestion is really just a "black box." Why is the charge of suggestion a nonexplanation?

ES: Nobody knows what the psychological mechanism of suggestibility is. Either you are suggestible or you aren't. Nobody really knows why. It has a genetic component, as some research demonstrates, but that's only part of the story. How you open holes in the black box is still very much a mystery. Today, in the neurosciences and in psychiatry, psychosomatic illnesses are almost as much a mystery as they were a hundred years ago. Nobody knows why they happen. It's clear that women were more subject to them than men. There is, as I said, a positive family history that makes you more likely to be a somatizer. But beyond those parameters, the whole business is a scientific quicksand. Physicians who get into it tend to vanish from the radar.

TD: Given your own interest in the biological perspective in psychiatry, I am curious to hear your thoughts about the biological Freud.

ES: I think it is very easy to overemphasize the biological elements in Freud's thought. Some of his partisans now, retrospectively, try to get psychoanalysis off the hook by saying that Freud recognized the bedrock of biology in his work. Freud said that maybe once in his life. The entire intellectual structure of psychoanalysis presupposes psychogenicity—that mental illnesses arise as a result of the action of the mind, as a result of unconscious conflicts. Freud's followers have always been fiercely opposed to the biological approach in psychiatry, and to psychopharmacology. So even though Freud passed on the idea that there may be something biological to be investigated, the whole analytic enterprise has been relentlessly hostile to biology.

TD: I certainly see a lot of biology in Freud's work, both before and after 1897.

ES: He doesn't really resume these ideas after 1900.

TD: Sure he does. The late texts, beginning with *Beyond the Pleasure Principle* [1920], are full of biology. Take a look at *Civilization and Its Discontents* [1930], which recalls the phylogenetic fantasies of *Totem and Taboo* [1913].

ES: But that speculative physical anthropology owes nothing at all to neurochemistry or brain biology. He had no interest in neuroanatomy, and there was no neurochemistry in his time. He had no interest in genetics, and later psychoanalysts have relentlessly denied the influence of genetics.

So saying that Freud was interested in phylogenesis doesn't make him a biological psychiatrist.

TD: Following Frank Sulloway [1979], I think that he kept the biology as an implicit foundation for his work.

ES: Lots of things may be implicit. Freud studied as a biologically oriented neurologist and not as a psychiatrist. So it's unsurprising to find isolated eruptions of interest in his work in neurobiology. For example, he saw a lot of neurosyphilitics, where the biology of their complaints was clear. And Freud never claimed that all psychiatric symptoms were psychogenic. However, his followers in particular resolutely turned their backs on neurobiology, psychopharmacology, psychiatric genetics, and anything else that has remotely organic seed.

So again I'd say that, even though Freud was a neurologist, not a psychiatrist, he had close to zero interest in neuroanatomy, neurochemistry, or genetics. Absent those, you can't claim that Freud had a red-hot curiosity about neurobiology.

TD: In your 1997 essay on Freud's Anna O., you attend carefully to the social and cultural context which made her symptoms possible. For example, you attend to her Jewish identity. How dangerous is it for a historian to emphasize such details?

ES: I think the Jewishness of Freud's milieu helps us explain the extraordinary number of people who believed they had something wrong with them. A kind of mental and physical hypochondriasis was built into the Jewish culture of Eastern Europe and had been there for hundreds of years, and it's interesting to see its periodic manifestations. Nerve doctors like Freud were able to capitalize on that sort of anxious self-preoccupation by telling women that they had hysteria, or men that they had neurasthenia—where in fact there was nothing wrong with them. I believe that the majority of Freud's patients were normal, that their illnesses were socially cultivated and were to some extent iatrogenic, as Freud, searching for the unconscious roots of their behavior, managed to convince them that they had medical illnesses.

To what extent are these considerations anti-Semitic? I don't think they are any more anti-Semitic than talking about the problems of American blacks under slavery, or problems of Polish miners in Minnesota. Canada and the United States are a patchwork quilt of ethnic groups, and each group has its own characteristics. Probably each ethnic group has its own characteristic illnesses and patterns of health seeking. To say that this is somehow "anti-" that ethnic group is absurd. So I don't see these considerations as dangerous at all. It is rather an obligation that academics have to tell the truth and not to pander to social prejudices.

TD: Sure. But it can be easy to mistake the description for a prescription.

ES: Too bad! My advice to the reader is to deal with it.

TD: In your book *From the Mind into the Body*, you devote one section to ethnic characteristics but then only speak about Jewish identity.

ES: It's a short book! I could have written about other ethnic groups, but I had spent all this time studying the Jews of Vienna and that was the ethnic group that I knew about.

TD: I'm not trying to suggest anything untoward, but am simply interested in any possible reaction you received from such passages.

ES: None that I'm aware of. But there was a significant German reaction to my *History of Psychiatry*. And, yes, some Germans deplored it as being anti-Semitic simply because I talk about these matters in a frank way. The Germans, of course, are totally unable to consider these issues with any kind of objectivity at all. So when they encounter such objectivity on the international scene, they shrink back in horror. I was reproached several times by German book reviewers for what they perceived as anti-Semitism. Incidentally, the German translation was made by a Jewish woman, who later told me that she would have been horrified by any hint of anti-Semitism and would never have translated the book. She certainly didn't see it.

TD: Did you respond to your critics?

ES: Somewhat, yes. I had a nasty little exchange with a Swiss psychiatrist, and the Swiss Psychiatric Association, over the whole issue of Max Müller and whether or not he himself was anti-Semitic. Müller was a very distinguished Swiss psychiatrist who flourished in the 1930s, and he made some absolutely coruscating remarks about Jewish colleagues, referring to them as typical Eastern European Jews. I said, in a footnote of the *History of Psychiatry*, that this was anti-Semitic, and his son, Christian, went through the roof when he saw it. In response, he managed to convince the Swiss Psychiatric Association, of which he is a leading member, to file a condemnation of me and my book. Later an article appeared in a Swiss Jewish weekly that was sympathetic to me and critical of Müller and the association. So I have indeed had my fingers burned on this anti-Semitism issue—and in a very surprising way.

TD: Elaine Showalter has said that she required bodyguards after publishing her work on hysteria, and received death threats from supporters of chronic fatigue. How have you fared with your critics?

ES: Over the years, I've had a fair amount of hate mail. And I've had people demonstrating outside my lectures. However, this has not deterred me from pressing on. I'm sorry that these people don't like my work, but we are paid to be academics. That means we should try to find out the truth, whether it's universally popular or not.

TD: Why is the work threatening?

ES: There are people suffering from diseases of the month, such as fibromyalgia, chronic fatigue syndrome, multiple chemical sensitivities, who have a huge psychological commitment to their diagnoses, and cannot stand to hear people say that the problems lack organicity and are due to somatization. In short, they have built up their entire lives on the fiction of organicity. So that's why they react so furiously when someone like myself comes along and, while recognizing their suffering, nonetheless doesn't go along with the diagnosis.

TD: What is the future of academic research in the history of medicine, and in psychoanalysis in particular?

ES: The history of medicine is really a growth field, probably where immunology was in the 1950s. The field is ready to just explode in the firmament of the humanities and social sciences. It's a field that has something very new to say about the human condition. As for the history of psychoanalysis, I think it's going to die out. As people lose interest in psychoanalysis in the real world, there is less and less curiosity about its history. And who cares?

TD: And for academics?

ES: I'm not discouraging the legitimacy of work on the history of psychoanalysis. But it is striking that, for decades now, nobody has had anything really new to say about the history of psychoanalysis. There haven't been any new texts.

TD: There are new letters.

ES: Well, they don't turn up very often. But, grosso modo, the texts people cite today are the same ones they were citing in the 1960s. This is not a field moving forward on the basis of new evidence. I think the history of psychoanalysis will come to have roughly the same interest to other investigators as the history of astrology has to us now.

TD: So the "death of psychoanalysis" has not been exaggerated?

ES: You must be kidding. Psychoanalysis today is dead within medicine and will shortly have, even in departments of English, the same intellectual status as Esperanto.

4

Psychoanalysis and Pseudoscience: Frank J. Sulloway Revisits Freud and His Legacy

Interviewed by Mikkel Borch-Jacobsen

Frank Sulloway received his PhD from Harvard University in 1978 and from 1984–1989 was a MacArthur Foundation fellow. He is currently visiting scholar at the Institute of Personality and Social Research and visiting professor in the Department of Psychology at Berkeley.

Sulloway is widely known among Freud scholars for his comprehensive book of 1979, *Freud, Biologist of the Mind: Beyond the Psychoanalytic Legend.* In this now-classic book, Sulloway provides the first sustained analysis of the role of biology in Freud's work and punctures the widespread claim that Freud was a misunderstood genius working in "splendid isolation." Based on his penetrating reading of Freud's early correspondence with his close friend and ally, Wilhelm Fliess, and on primary research in the history of science, Sulloway cut through decades of mystification about psychoanalysis and forever changed the course of Freud studies. Put simply, Sulloway returned Freud, who was, after all, trained as a neurologist, to his proper intellectual context: nineteenth-century science.

Sulloway has remained interested in psychoanalysis, writing the occasional essay, but has also moved on to his other interests in the history of science. His best-selling book, *Born to Rebel: Birth Order, Family Dynamics, and Creative Lives*, was published in 1996, and he is currently working on *In Darwin's Footsteps: Discovery and Change in the Galapagos Islands*. He also recently completed a several-year study of the adaptive significance of religion.

The interview with Mikkel Borch-Jacobsen took place in Boston on November 19, 1994, but was edited and updated in 2005. The interview is part of a joint project conceived in partnership with historian Sonu Shamdasani. Borch-Jacobsen himself is interviewed later in this book.

. . .

MB-J: *Freud, Biologist of the Mind: Beyond the Psychoanalytic Legend* marked an important date in Freud studies, not only due to its historical rigor and its impressive erudition, but also because it was in many respects the first overtly "revisionistic" interpretation of Freud and the origins of psychoanalysis. You yourself introduce this term in the first pages of the book, which has come to define the subsequent scholarship that has challenged the Freud legend. It was not that you were the first one to call into question this legend, forged by Freud and his biographer-disciples. Paul Roazen and Henri Ellenberger had already preceded you in taking on aspects of this legend. But you were without a doubt the first to have so clearly and overtly presented your historical work as a critique of psychoanalysis. At bottom, how did you, who are not a psychoanalyst, decide to write an intellectual biography of Freud? At the outset, were you favorable to psychoanalysis? Or did you begin this enormous work already with the idea of putting it in its place?

FS: Let me begin by telling you how I became interested in writing a book on Freud. I had always felt that one ought to know something about psychoanalysis, so when I graduated from Harvard College, in 1969, and was about to begin my graduate school education, I decided to read Ernest Jones's biography of Freud and some of Freud's principal works, such as *The Interpretation of Dreams* [1900]. One aspect that particularly puzzled me about Ernest Jones's biography was that he never really explained the origin of some of the most fundamental concepts of psychoanalysis, at least in the way a historian of science would do. These concepts are mostly taken for granted. The reason why Jones did this is that he assumed these concepts were fundamentally true, just like the laws of gravity: one doesn't really need to explain, in any great detail, how and why Isaac Newton became aware of gravity, for gravity obviously exists.

I wasn't satisfied by this approach. Many psychoanalytic assumptions, such as cathexis, organic repression, and childhood polymorphous perversity, for instance, are not intuitively obvious, and they struck me as having no adequate prehistory to them. So I read Freud's correspondence with his friend and colleague Wilhelm Fliess in the abridged and censored edition that was available at the time. In this correspondence I noticed references to what Freud called abandoned erotogenic zones—the notion that a child would find pleasure in oral and anal sensations, including the smell of feces—together with Freud's remarks that such abandoned erotogenic sensations have phylogenetic implications and links to zoophilia. I recognized these remarks as endorsing the basic assumption behind Haeckel's biogenetic law—namely, that the individual is destined to recapitulate the phylogenetic history of the species—and in this respect Freud's whole discussion made perfect sense to me. What particularly struck me, though, was that these discussions were taking place in December 1896 and January 1897—that is to say, about nine months before the supposed discovery of infantile sexuality during Freud's famous self-analysis. Now, how could Freud "discover" something that he had already been talking about for almost a year? It immediately struck me that these discussions about infantile sexuality were part of a dialogue with Fliess. A Berlin physician who specialized in nose-and-throat disorders, Fliess was also widely read in the field of biology, and he would have understood Freud's implicit endorsement of Haeckelian biogenetic thinking about human development.

Fliess's side of the correspondence is largely lost, but it is quite obvious from Freud's letters that he was not receiving letters back from Fliess saying, "How dare you talk about the child being sexual and having abandoned erotogenic zones!" Ernest Jones presents Freud as a man who made himself very unpopular by talking and writing about infantile sexuality, but this is certainly not the picture one gets from the correspondence with Fliess. Fliess is apparently taking infantile sexuality for granted, and he is a willing partner in this whole discussion.

Given the theoretical assumptions Fliess apparently shared with Freud, it becomes readily understandable why Fliess did not reject such ideas. In Fliess's case, these shared assumptions had also led him to propose that all life is regulated by two sexual rhythms—a 28-day female cycle and a 23-day male cycle [Fliess 1897]. Whether one thinks Fliess's specific ideas are right or wrong—and we now know them to be mostly wrong, especially about the supposed male cycle—it is clear that he shared with Freud the conviction that all life is regulated by sexuality, and hence by sexual chemistry. In Fliess's 1897 book, which Freud read in manuscript in 1896, before his self-analysis, Fliess had argued that the child's date of birth is determined by the fluctuations of these two sexual cycles. Fliess also claimed that major stages in childhood development were influenced by these cycles, so it was perfectly natural for him to believe in infantile sexuality.

Now here I was, face-to-face with an interesting problem as a young historian of science. I had come across a famous intellectual "discovery" occurring nine months before it is supposed to have taken place in Freud's life. I had also come to understand that this discovery had emerged in the context of a collaborative relationship between two people, one of whom—Wilhelm Fliess—had been consistently maligned by Freud's biographers for his pseudoscientific views about periodicity and bisexuality, and whose deductions about infantile sexuality had never been mentioned in any previous biographical writings about Freud.

When I came to this realization in the early 1970s, I thought this to be a very strange state of affairs, so I did something that few people had probably done since the Freud-Fliess letters came out in the German-language edition of 1950. I went back and read Wilhelm Fliess's original works. Lo and behold, there I found references to the child having erections at 23- and 28-day intervals, to thumb-sucking being a substitute form of sexuality, and so forth. My God, I thought, this material suggests a completely different view of the origins of one of Freud's most fundamental insights—the existence of infantile sexuality! So I started to write a short paper on this topic. It grew into a long paper, then into a short book, then into a medium-sized book, and eventually into the fairly substantial book I finally published in 1979.

The reason why my manuscript kept growing is because this biogenetic way of thinking about sexuality, far from being a single, accidental episode in Freud's intellectual development, turned out to be a pervasive and unifying theme in the development of his overall psychoanalytic theorizing. The more I followed the thread of these particular conceptual threads throughout Freud's life and thought, the more I realized that the psychobiological paradigm that Freud and Fliess had shared in the 1890s was a mode of thinking that had subsequently sent its tentacles through the entire creation of psychoanalysis as we know it. I found myself in an odd situation, for I had no intention initially of writing a book on Freud. Once I got started, however, the book essentially wrote itself.

As soon as I realized there was a fundamental discrepancy in the traditional historical accounts of how Freud made his most important discoveries, this conclusion opened up Pandora's box, as it were. You asked before about my original attitude toward Freud, and I would have to say that the writing of my book radically transformed my thinking about him. When I began the book, I approached Freud, as most people did at the time, as one of the great minds of the twentieth century, somebody on a par with Copernicus and Darwin, as he himself once claimed. But the more I looked into the development of psychoanalysis, the more I discovered that it was based on outmoded nineteenth-century assumptions that were clearly refuted by the rediscovery of Mendel's laws in genetics, by the overthrow of Lamarckian theory in evolutionary biology, and by the rejection of the various Helmholtzian physiological assumptions that were crucial to Freud's thinking about hysteria, and neurotic symptom formation more generally.

So when I finally finished this book, I found myself somewhat reluctantly having to admit that Freud was not the great discoverer I—and many others—had thought. I became, in spite of myself, a critic not only of psychoanalytic theory but also of what I increasingly saw as the politically motivated act of construction, by Freud and his followers, of a historical legend to prevent this view of Freud from being widely understood. In this general critique of the Freud legend, I was, of course, following a path on which others had gone before me, in particular Henri Ellenberger, on whom I drew considerably in my book.

MB-J: How was the book received?

FS: On publication, my book was widely perceived as a far-reaching critique of the validity of psychoanalysis, although I still had to admire Freud for the sweep of his overall intellectual creation. Had the outmoded biological assumptions on which he built his psychoanalytic edifice been correct, then psychoanalytic theory might well have been mostly correct. I tried to treat Freud, in my book, the way a historian of science would treat Aristotle and any other great thinkers of the past who were now known to be mostly in error in their scientific theories. This particular historical approach, incidentally, seeks to avoid the fallacy of Whiggish history, or the tendency to write history from the perspective of how it all finally turned out. It was a methodological perspective I had been taught in graduate school. For example, historians of science were then trying to write the history of pseudosciences, such as phrenology, without being overly dismissive of these intellectual pursuits, given the obvious evidence of their ultimate scientific failure. In hindsight, I've come to realize that such an anti-Whiggish historical approach has its own limitations, because I was in many ways too kind to Freud and sometimes wrote about his "insights" and "discoveries" without specifically stating that I did not personally believe these specific insights and discoveries to be valid. Frederick Crews [1986, 88–111] later took me to task for using such language, and he was right to do so, although he himself, I think, sometimes went too far and occasionally committed the fallacy of Whiggish history in his own criticisms of Freud.

Since I wrote my book on Freud, I have become, as you know, even more critical of Freud's theories and legacy. Much of this subsequent critique is already implicit in my book, but it was not developed as clearly as it should have been, in part because of my attempt to avoid the fallacy of Whiggish history. In any event, I have come to see psychoanalysis much more clearly as something of a tragedy, as a discipline that evolved from a very promising science into a very disappointing pseudoscience. Science is a two-step process. The first step is the development of hypotheses, and at this stage it doesn't really matter whether one's hypotheses are right or wrong. In other words, Freud could afford to have a lot of erroneous hypotheses based on ideas and assumptions that were current in his day but that later turned out not to be true. This is not the failing point of good science. Where science more often goes wrong is during the second step, which consists of testing one's hypotheses and giving them up if they turn out to be wrong. This second step is much more crucial, in fact, than the first one, for one can afford to be mistaken during the first step only so long as one is extremely rigorous during the second step.

The more I studied psychoanalysis, especially in its clinical practice as described by Freud in his famous case histories, the more I came to the conclusion that Freud had developed a set of extremely compelling, extremely plausible hypotheses for his day, but that he never took that key, second procedural step in the rigorous manner that is required for true science. Science is not just a set of facts and theories but also a method, a way of questioning what one thinks is true. And it's in its faulty methodology that psychoanalysis has met its ultimate downfall.

MB-J: You claim in your book that Fliess's theories on bisexuality and infantile sexuality had a completely determining influence on Freud. You also argue that it was with these ideas from Fliess that Freud could fill the void left by the collapse of his seduction theory and substitute it with a theory of sexuality of biological inspiration. Would you go so far as saying that it was Fliess who was the veritable instigator of that which we call Freudian psychoanalysis?

FS: No, I wouldn't—and I didn't say that in my book. In my book, I described the relationship between Fliess's ideas on infantile sexuality and what became of them in psychoanalytic theory in terms of a transformation. The title of one of my chapters is "Freud's Psychoanalytic Transformation of the Fliessian Id." Freud clearly saw implications in this psychobiological view of infancy that Fliess had not, and this was a very creative transformation indeed—which doesn't say anything, by the way, about whether it was right or wrong. However, the core assumptions of Freud's theory of sexuality, and psychosexual development more generally, clearly drew on ideas that he shared with Fliess and in some cases derived directly from him.

Indeed, these Fliessian assumptions were crucial to salvaging Freud's theory of human sexual development and of psychopathology, once the seduction theory fell apart. If neuroses are not due to childhood sexual traumas—to "seductions," as Freud called them—but rather to endogenous, internal impulses that either do or do not undergo repression, this new way of thinking obviously throws the emphasis back onto the spontaneous nature of sexuality in the child. This is clearly a biological view about human sexual development; and indeed, in his later works, Freud more than once pointed out the parallels between the psychoanalytic view of the endogenous nature of infantile sexuality and Fliess's own biological theories. Like Fliess, Freud explicitly wrote about infantile psychosexual development in terms of the periodic ebb and flow of sexuality in a child, and he also proposed that night terrors in children, which he believed to be caused by improperly channeled libido, occurred at regular, 28-day intervals. Whether or not Freud believed in the correctness of Fliess's theories in later years is unimportant, although there is no evidence that Freud ever abandoned his belief that Fliess was right about the fundamental role of periodic developmental "thrusts" in infancy and life more generally.

What ultimately mattered for Freud and psychoanalysis is that Fliess's way of thinking about human development as being biologically driven was crucial to the new view of human development that Freud adopted once the seduction theory and his predominantly environmentalist interpretation of neurosis fell through in 1897. In fact, Fliess's views must have helped to undermine Freud's confidence in that erroneous theory. The resulting change in Freud's thinking involves extensive intellectual borrowing, and the fact that Freud developed these ideas into a vast intellectual system doesn't minimize his considerable debt to this Fliessian way of thinking.

Could Freud have done it without Fliess? It is difficult to second-guess history, and it is also true that Freud was himself sufficiently versed in evolutionary and biogenetic views of life to have reached the same series of insights by himself. But it certainly didn't hurt for him to have someone actively pushing these key biological perspectives at a time when he desperately needed an alternative to his failed explanations for neuroses. In the history of science, there is clearly an important distinction between ideas just being out there and one's best friend touting these very same ideas that later became central to Freud's own theories of human development and the origins of the psychoneuroses.

MB-J: Psychoanalysts claim that Freud drew his ideas from two sources: from clinical observation of his patients and from his famous self-analysis. By contrast, you show the decisive role of Freud's reading, which, at the very least, greatly qualifies the decisive role that has been attributed to the former sources and further raises the suspicion whether the latter, rather than being a world-historical act of introspection, largely consisted of a prolonged sojourn in the library. How do you view the significance attributed to Freud's self-analysis in the genesis of psychoanalysis?

FS: I have always felt that self-analysis was not the fundamental cause of Freud's abandonment of the seduction theory or of his subsequent theoretical developments. The handwriting was on the wall. Fliess's biological viewpoint, the evidence from sexology, the disappointing clinical evidence from his own quasi disciple, Felix Gattel, who had been working up case histories from a Freudian perspective in Richard von Krafft-Ebing's clinic, and so forth—all these different sorts of negative evidence indicated that the seduction theory just wasn't true. Rather than discovering that unwelcome truth in his self-analysis, Freud essentially read into his self-analysis what he had already begun to realize from these other sources of evidence.

MB-J: Fliess would later accuse Freud of reading his own mind into his patients'.[1] Are you saying that, in this instance, Freud read Wilhelm Fliess's, Richard von Krafft-Ebing's, Albert Moll's, and other sexologists' theories into his own mind?

FS: Yes, I would say he did just that. How is it possible, in a self-analysis, not to be conditioned by all the scientific knowledge, reading, and diverse evidence that a person like Freud has gathered from numerous other researches and disciplines? How could one possibly prevent those relevant sources of information from steering one's self-analysis in a certain direction? If one begins to read in the scientific literature that the infant is much more sexually spontaneous than one had ever thought, how could one not decide to probe that issue in one's own self-analysis? So it shouldn't come as a big surprise if Freud, during his self-analysis, supposedly uncovered a memory of having seen his mother naked at the age of two. If some of the books Freud was reading were telling him similar things, and if he then discovered such experiences in his own childhood, well, big news! It's obvious, and hardly profound.

In traditional Freud scholarship, the self-analysis has been made into a causal agent of Freud's originality, but that historical scenario is simply not true. Ideas that were supposedly derived from the self-analysis are credited for many of Freud's most important intellectual discoveries, but we now know that those ideas were generally derived from somewhere else and were definitely not the product of the self-analysis per se. The self-analysis is one of the great legendary stories in the history of science. Although Freud himself really didn't spawn this aspect of the Freud legend, it is interesting to note that he did nothing to prevent it from spreading.

It was Fritz Wittels who first claimed, in his 1924 biography of Freud, that Freud must have discovered infantile sexuality in the course of his self-analysis. Freud read that biography very carefully and corrected various errors in it, but he did not correct this one. The reason he didn't, I think, is that he rather liked the story. It clearly was not true, but it was the kind of biographical story that ought to have been true according to psychoanalytic theory and the legend its theory entails.

1. "The reader of thoughts merely reads his own thoughts into the other people" (in Masson 1985, 446).

MB-J: You are a historian of ideas, and at bottom you seem to hold that ideas engender one another in a continuous sequence. Some people believe in radical scientific "revolutions" or "breaks." Hence, in the case of psychoanalysis, simply because Freud took a concept from Fliess, Krafft-Ebing, or Albert Moll doesn't mean that he is speaking of the same thing these other people were. This line of thinking is very fashionable amongst French psychoanalysts of Lacanian inspiration, and Elisabeth Roudinesco [1986] explicitly poses it against you as follows: "Sulloway forgets a fundamental epistemological fact: Freud is not content with establishing what everyone else knows in 'stealing' ideas from his contemporaries, he translated facts through new concepts . . . In accusing him of falsifying history, Sulloway reasons, despite his great erudition, as if theory was of the same nature as concrete facts, as if the concept of a dog was produced by barking. This type of argumentation is frequent, and has to be put back in history, as one of the forms of the resistance to the Freudian discovery. This consists in demonstrating that Freud invented nothing, and that of which he speaks existed before him, like the most shared thing of the world" [32–33]. How do you reply to this?

FS: This is an interesting historiographical issue, and a delicate one as well. At the simplest level, I would answer your question this way: if one totally believes in psychoanalysis and one thinks Freud is a genius, then everything he did is seen to be revolutionary, and any parallels with his predecessors have to be the product of an amazing transformation of ideas, of a radical rupture from the past. The more one reveres Freud, the more one is bound to endorse a revolutionary model of history. By contrast, if one is critical of Freud and psychoanalysis, it is natural to see the history of psychoanalysis as an evolutionary process, with substantial intellectual debts to previous thinkers.

Now, in the quotation from Roudinesco that you just cited, I am portrayed in a rather extreme historiographical manner as claiming that Freud lifted hook, line, and sinker most of his ideas from other people. I certainly didn't say this in my book, and I went to great lengths in my book to show the many ways in which psychoanalysis synthesized existing ideas and then transformed them in interesting ways. Roudinesco is attacking a straw man—a position I have never held. Again, one of the fundamental chapters of my book deals with "Freud's Psychoanalytic Transformation of the Fliessian Id." There is no revolution in the history of science where there is complete conceptual discontinuity; there is always some degree of transformation, as I. Bernard Cohen [1985] has persuasively argued. As historians of science have generally come to appreciate in their study of other great scientific innovators, such as Galileo, Newton, and Darwin, an evolutionary model of history is almost always closer to the truth than a revolutionary one—even for revolutionary thinkers. So it's really a question of exactly where we put Freud on a scale extending from total borrowing of preexisting ideas to radical innovation.

Personally, I would put Freud somewhere in the middle on such a scale of originality, but rather closer to the original end than the unoriginal end of the scale. I give him tremendous credit for having transformed old ideas in new ways, even though most of these new ways of thinking were not scientifically correct. Psychoanalysis is an impressive synthesis of ideas from the late nineteenth century, and nobody else had put all these ideas together in quite the same powerful way that Freud did. If we lived in a Lamarckian world rather than in a Darwinian world, if the inheritance of acquired characteristics was really possible, and if energy really did circulate in the body according to a Helmholtzian, hydraulic model so that unused libidinal energy could become diverted and cause neurophysiological disturbances—in a word, if all of these mistaken biological notions were true, it is quite possible that psychoanalytic theory would, in large part, be true. The problem is that these assumptions are not true. The discipline of psychoanalysis was built on intellectual quicksand, and it has been sinking ever since.

In any event, if people write on the subject of Freud's originality from a loyalist psychoanalytic perspective, they will almost always defend the "rupture" view of history, and they will tend to portray anyone else who takes the evolutionary view as trying to wheedle Freud's originality down in an unflattering manner. That kind of disagreement is part of the politics of the historiographical discipline. Incidentally, I tried to analyze this politics at length in my book, devoting a chapter to "The Myth of the Hero" and attempting to show in this chapter how Freud and his followers touted a revolutionary model of history in an effort to enhance his originality and to insulate psychoanalysis from its origins in outmoded nineteenth-century psychobiology.

MB-J: Following up on this last point, you affirm in your book that psychoanalysis is not the purely psychological theory that Freud and his successors wished to depict it as. On the contrary, you state that there is a profound continuity between the initially neurophysiological and biological preoccupations of Freud and the complex psychobiology that he elaborated under the name of psychoanalysis. If what you say in your book is true, how, then, could everyone be persuaded that Freud was a pure psychologist who had broken with the biologism of his contemporaries? How did this legend establish itself? And why?

FS: This is a very interesting question because it goes to the heart of the politics of the psychoanalytic movement and the way this movement has sought to portray itself and its history. It is fair to say that if one goes through the *Standard Edition* of Freud's works, one can find him making every possible statement about the conceptual relationship between psychoanalysis and biology. So depending upon what position one wants to take, as a psychoanalyst or as a critic of psychoanalysis, one will find at one's disposal all of the seemingly compelling quotations from Freud that one needs to support one's position. The real question is, why is Freud saying all these obviously contradictory things? When somebody says things that are so contradictory, one has to wonder what is really going on.

The most straightforward answer to this question is that Freud was incredibly ambivalent about the whole issue, and this ambivalence clearly had to do with his troubled relationship with Fliess, with whom he shared a profound desire to unite biology with psychology in an effort to understand human development. As Robert Merton [1976] has shown, ambivalence is a hallmark of scientists' attitudes toward priority. Scientists try to be modest and humble, but they also seek to gain maximum credit for their ideas. Freud's relationship to Fliess was filled with such intense ambivalence over matters relating to priority. The relationship with Fliess is not the only source of Freud's ambivalence about his extensive intellectual debts to biology, but it certainly made a major contribution to it. Freud was also ambivalent about biology for another good reason. His often speculative biological assumptions risked refutation by the progress of science.

Just think of it: Freud had gotten himself into a richly collaborative relationship with this really smart guy who had a lot of provocative and novel ideas about human sexual chemistry, sexual periodicity, bisexuality, and even infantile sexuality that were all helping Freud to solve some of the most significant theoretical problems he was facing at the time. All of a sudden the issue comes down to, hey, who deserves the most credit? By 1901, we know that matters had gotten to the point where Freud was willing to offer coauthorship to Fliess of what became the *Three Essays on the Theory of Sexuality* if that enticement would ensure continuation of the collaboration [see Masson 1985, 448]. In his letter offering Fliess coauthorship, Freud states that he is planning to entitle this book *Bisexuality in Man.* Clearly, one does not offer coauthorship of one of one's most famous books to somebody else unless one has really merged minds with that person, owes this other person a substantial intellectual debt, and, as was true of Freud, needs this person's continuing assistance with as-yet unsolved problems. The subsequent estrangement between Freud and Fliess prevented this collaborative publication. But the evidence of its far-reaching impact on psychoanalysis is documented in my book, and is based on Freud's correspondence with Fliess, Freud's various published references to Fliess's theories, and Fliess's own published references to Freud's work.

After the break with Fliess occurred, Freud discovered that many of his early followers, such as Stekel and Adler, were also reading Fliess's works—and similar works by other psychobiologically oriented authors. One has to understand that Freud and Fliess were not the only guys in town playing the game of trying to reduce psychology to biology and trying to show how one can fruitfully cross from one field to the other. This was the intellectual game of the late nineteenth century—the game of the Helmholtz school of medicine and later an increasingly Darwinian game, including a game played by many of the people in the emerging field of sexual psychopathology. Trying to unite psychology with biology was an exciting intellectual strategy to pursue, and people are still pursuing it today; for one cannot base a theory of the mind on pure psychology. Such a theory of mind has to have some roots in developmental biology, genetics, neurophysiology, and evolutionary biology.

Freud, of course, knew this because he was trained as a biologist. But with some of his early disciples trying to create alternative schools of psychoanalysis based on their own use of Fliess's and other contemporary researchers' psychobiological works, Freud soon realized that his own previous mining of this intellectual treasure trove was a double-edged sword. If everybody continued to do what he had done by building on biological bedrock, one might soon have a myriad of different forms of psychoanalysis, and then what would become of Freud's own originality and, especially, his intellectual hegemony in psychoanalysis? Freud therefore decided that the safest thing to do was to tell his disciples that psychoanalysis needed to become a pure psychology. One of the most amazing things is that most of these disciples bought into this requirement; or at least this perspective was generally accepted by those disciples who remained within Freud's circle. These followers really did believe that psychoanalysis was a purely psychological discipline in which the principal sources of evidence are patients on the couch and whatever subjective, self-analytic material one can cull from oneself or from the personal experiences of one's colleagues. This new emphasis on psychoanalysis as a pure psychology, and hence on the discipline being independent of other fields of inquiry, really helped to prevent dissension. I was just rereading the other day Freud's 1926 essay, "The Question of Lay Analysis," in which he proposes to divorce psychoanalytic education from training within medical schools. Now why would he want to do that? Medical schools are the place where medicine has always been taught. But such schools are also the same places where one learns biology and other relevant fields of natural science, which are the cornerstone of modern medicine. Because biology was a constant threat to Freud, the easiest way for him to minimize that threat was for him to privatize psychoanalytic training, to take it out of the medical schools, and to induce his disciples to believe that psychoanalysis is a pure psychology that stands apart from other disciplines and so does not have to answer to them. This strategy did not prevent Freud from going back to biology whenever he felt like it, such as when he developed his ideas about the death instinct in 1920. Like many creative people, Freud told his disciples one thing and then did another himself. But Freud's strategy did immunize his theories from subsequent and much-needed revision when the assumptions on which he had built his psychoanalytic edifice underwent significant revision in the fields from which he had drawn.

Freud's ambivalence toward biology explains why every possible statement about the relationship between biology and psychoanalysis can be found in Freud's collected works. To make sense out of such conflicting statements, one needs to know who the audience is for this or that particular statement.

MB-J: In your view, were all these legends we have been talking about deliberately fabricated by Freud and his successors? Could one go further and speak of dishonesty as regards the manner in which Freud rewrote his own history?

FS: As a historian of science who has studied the lives of eminent scientists such as Copernicus, Galileo, Newton, and Darwin, I am familiar with numerous legends by which to compare the legend about Freud. From this perspective, I will unhesitatingly say that no legend in the history of science has ever been developed in such elaborate ways as the legend fostered by psychoanalysts about its own origins. Psychoanalysis is the only theory in the history of science that demands that its own history be absolutely consistent with the theory developed by its originator. Darwin did not claim, for example, that the discovery of natural selection was the result of a "natural selection" of ideas going on in his head. Newton never claimed that his thoughts "gravitated" toward the theory of universal gravitation. But psychoanalysis demands that the life of its founder—especially his childhood and the heroic, self-analytic path he supposedly took to his discoveries—agree with major tenets of the theory. From a historiographical perspective, this kind of circular logic can get one into a lot of trouble. If Freud's theories were 100 percent true, one might perhaps be able to produce a reasonably good history using this conceptual approach. But, to the extent that the theory is problematic, one is bound to end up with a problematic history—and, most likely, a badly flawed, self-serving history.

This extraordinary requirement—that the history of the theory's origins be explained by the actual theory—created a problem for the history of psychoanalysis that has never been faced by any other discipline in the entire history of science. In this connection, let me now address your related question: to what extent is the psychoanalytic legend tendentious? As I have said, the Freud legend certainly is more fully developed and more politically motivated than any other legend in the history of science, so we can definitely see the hand of motivated distortion in its history. Keep in mind that psychoanalysis was under heavy scientific attack as this legend was taking form. The legend was part of the movement's defense mechanisms. Of course, one might argue that this circumstance was also true of other controversial theories, such as Darwinism. But Darwinism triumphed: people soon realized Darwin was right, and no serious scientist nowadays doubts the fundamental truth of evolutionary theory. Although legends did arise about Darwin, they were never essential to protecting his theories, to immunizing them from criticism. As a discipline, psychoanalysis never succeeded in the way Darwin's theories have done, and the role of the Freud legend has therefore remained politically expedient in the discipline, which also means that there is more motivation, even today, for partisans of this theory to cross the line into tendentious uses of history.

I am not saying, though, that Freud and his disciples sat around a table and deliberately decided to lie about their history. The process was much more subtle. In some cases, these various component myths that make up the Freud legend—of which I have identified more than twenty in my book—were almost innocent because, in the context of psychoanalytic theory, they seemed so plausible. At any rate, such myths were generally not explicitly dishonest. But such legendary forms of history did involve pervasive self-deception. Whenever self-deception is involved, it is always hard to know how much it includes outright dishonesty, as Allen Esterson [1993] has noted about Freud's often blatantly false clinical assertions. This issue is like asking whether there was dishonesty in the bitter political fights that went on in the French National Convention, during the French Revolution, when these deputies portrayed each other in highly distorted ways and often sent each other to the guillotine. The point is that each side believed its own distortions. A. A. Brill has described the ways in which the early disciples at Bleuler's Burghölzli Mental Clinic would analyze each other every time one of them did anything out of the ordinary, such as dropping a spoon or forgetting a name. Well, when one is writing one's own history in this same fashion, living and breathing the theory that informs one's entire sense of history, one is bound to come up with dubious and self-serving conclusions.

MB-J: Is psychoanalysis allergic to history?

FS: Yes, well put. Psychoanalysts do seem to have antibodies toward history, and one important reason is that, in psychoanalysis, nothing is supposed to be the way it seems. The manifest content of thoughts and dreams, for example, is always just a superficial, distorted layer of the latent, or hidden, content. So the job of a psychoanalyst who approaches history is often to show how most of what a nonpsychoanalytic historian has ever written about the subject—whether it is the history of the psychoanalytic movement or some other aspect of psychohistory—has missed the point and is therefore wrong. So far, the rather dismal record of psychohistory, as David Stannard [1980] has shown, is largely a record of gross distortions and embarrassing historiographical failures.

If a fundamental tenet of one's "scientific" way of thinking is that nothing is the way it seems, one soon gets to a point where nothing can be proved, for no evidence can ever be trusted—except the evidence that confirms what one already believes. If I produced compelling historical evidence about, say, some idea that Freud derived from Richard von Krafft-Ebing, the average psychoanalyst who wanted to defend Freud's originality might think: "Ah, but that's only superficial evidence—manifest-content evidence! Since Freud's use of that idea he supposedly derived from Krafft-Ebing was substantially different once Freud developed his revolutionary psychoanalytic vision, Freud is really an original genius, not an intellectual pilferer. So, you see, it's not at all what it seems." Unfortunately, psychoanalytic reasoning is too circular for its practitioners to correct such self-serving accounts of history, or go beyond them.

MB-J: Tell me a bit more about how your views regarding Freud and psychoanalysis have changed over the years since you wrote your 1979 book.

FS: When I undertook my book on Freud in the mid-1970s, I researched and wrote it as a historian of ideas. I approached psychoanalytic theory as an intellectual system, tried to show where these ideas came from, sought to trace and dissect the various conceptual components that Freud adapted from other people's work, and attempted to support my historical assertions by a detailed study of Freud's marginalia in his personal library, and so forth. But I didn't tackle psychoanalysis as a system of clinical treatment or as a form of scientific training. A decade later, it had become much clearer in my mind that my failure to include a chapter on psychoanalysis as a clinical method, and also as a form of medical education and practice, represented a significant omission from my book, which is something that I acknowledged in a 1991 article on Freud's case histories. Indeed, when one looks closely at psychoanalysis as a form of clinical practice, one is bound—in my view at least—to become much more critical of Freud's achievements and legacy.

As I stated earlier, science is a two-step process. The first step is to formulate reasonably plausible hypotheses—the best one can propose under the circumstances. The second step, which is the really crucial one, is to test these hypotheses and to accept defeat when they are shown to be incorrect. This is an extraordinarily difficult thing for human beings to do, and it took a revolution in science in the seventeenth century—the so-called scientific revolution—to develop an intellectual technology that was ultimately accepted by the entire scientific community in an effort to make its practitioners more self-critical about the foundations of scientific knowledge. This is an intellectual technology that consists of constantly throwing all one's pet theories to the wall, so to speak, and it is something that people do not learn without extensive professional guidance and training. Even with such training, the scientific method is difficult to implement, because we always tend to favor our own hypotheses, as Darwin once pointed out. In his *Autobiography*, Darwin noted that he had tried to follow "a golden rule, namely, that whenever a published fact, a new observation or thought came across me which was opposed to my general results, to make a memorandum of it without fail and at once; for I had found by experience that such facts and thoughts were far more apt to escape from the memory than favourable ones" [Darwin 1958]. Unlike Darwin, Freud was less scrupulous about following this "golden rule," and his faulty clinical methods also continuously undermined his ability to do so.

Controversy over Freud's theories only made matters worse. What did the field of psychoanalysis do, during its early years, when it ran into trouble—that is, when it was confronted by ever-mounting criticisms from psychiatrists, psychologists, and people in the biological fields from which Freud had borrowed so extensively? The field reacted regressively by privatizing its training mechanisms, which means that it took itself out of that enormously successful tradition, which first emerged during the scientific revolution, of testing theories using formal methods of self-criticism. Instead, the discipline of psychoanalysis took a step back toward scholasticism and the medieval tradition that preceded the scientific revolution by founding small private institutes in which knowledge could be transmitted dogmatically and where students were taught how to overcome their "resistances" to the theory. Edward Glover [1952], who directed research at the London Institute of Psychoanalysis for sixteen years, has highlighted the enormous pitfalls of the training analysis:

It is scarcely to be expected that a student who has spent some years under the artificial and sometimes hothouse conditions of a training analysis and whose professional career depends on overcoming "resistance" to the satisfaction of his training analyst, can be in a favorable position to defend his scientific integrity against his analyst's theory and practice. And the longer he remains in training analysis, the less likely he is to do so. For according to his analyst the candidate's objections to interpretations rate as "resistances." In short, there is a tendency inherent in the training situation to perpetuate error.

If you think about it even for a moment, this form of education is the most astonishing reversal of everything that Copernicus, Kepler, Galileo,

Newton, and the entire scientific revolution fought for! Once I fully appreciated how regressive a step this was, seen in historical context, I decided to look at Freud's own case histories to see to what extent he ever really tested his hypotheses. You see, as long as one concentrates on the first, or hypothesis formulation, stage of science, which is basically what I had done in my book, Freud looks pretty good. He was a genius at formulating plausible hypotheses, and he deserves an A for that achievement. But when it comes to the second, or testing, stage of science, he gets no more than a D– or even an E. He was personally responsible for the privatization of training mechanisms, and this privatization is equivalent to ceasing to test—in other words, for rejecting the hard-won scientific strictures of the last four centuries, and hence the most important achievement of the scientific revolution.

Psychoanalysis may have been a science in 1895 or perhaps even as late as in 1900, but by 1915 or 1920—that is, by the time it had developed the training analysis as a routine form of psychoanalytic education—the discipline could no longer claim to possess any real scientific pretensions. Through its rigid forms of training, psychoanalysis ceased to be a science, and when a discipline ceases to be a science, it becomes a pseudoscience. I have not the slightest doubt that psychoanalysis is a pseudoscience today. It's not that psychoanalytic theory is untestable, by the way. Many components of the overall theory are definitely testable, as Adolf Grünbaum [1984] has argued. The problem lies with the field's practitioners, who were not taught to test their theories in a scientific manner. So psychoanalysis per se is not technically a pseudoscience. Rather, its practitioners are mostly pseudoscientists—an important distinction, although the net result is that the field generally espouses pseudoscientific ideas and is unable to correct them.

MB-J: In the article you mention, you don't hesitate to put in doubt the veracity of all the great case histories of Freud, drawing on the damaging discrepancies brought to life by Morton Schatzman, Han Israëls, Zvi Lothane, Patrick Mahony, and Karin Obholzer, not to mention Paul Roazen, Ola Andersson, Henri Ellenberger, and Peter Swales. Was the great Freud a charlatan? To what extent can one still trust the veracity of the factual evidence that Freud marshals in support of psychoanalysis?

FS: I wrote my 1991 article on Freud's case histories partly as a missing chapter of my book, and partly because of a series of valuable studies that had appeared in the meantime on various specific case histories. In the light of this new and intriguing literature, I felt it was time for someone to try to synthesize what we had learned from it. So I am grateful to all those scholars you just mentioned for having done so much of the spade work, and to people like Frank Cioffi, Adolf Grünbaum, Frederick Crews, and Malcolm Macmillan, who have also made important contributions to our understanding of Freud's methodological shortcomings. What I tried to do in my article, based in large part on the research by these scholars, was to see whether there was some kind of larger pattern in these case histories, and indeed there was.

Previously, looking at Freud as a theoretician, I had not fully appreciated the extent of his arbitrariness as a practitioner and how wide a berth there was for him to interpret, in arbitrary ways, the reasons for anything said to him. Yes, I certainly did understand this point in a general way, as when I wrote in the concluding chapter of my Freud book: "Time and time again, Freud saw in his patients what psychoanalytic theory led him to look for and then to interpret the way he did; and when the theory changed, so did the clinical findings" [1979, 498]. But I simply did not do full justice, in my treatment of Freud, to detailing the faulty clinical and intellectual methods that underlay these flawed interpretations.

Here is just one clinical example, to give a sense as to what psychoanalytic interpretations by Freud were often like. Clarence Oberndorf went to see Freud around 1923 or 1924. Like all candidates for training under Freud, Oberndorf came in prepared with a dream. The dream involved driving in a carriage with a black horse and a white horse. Because Oberndorf came from the southern part of the United States, Freud interpreted the dream to mean that Oberndorf had an inhibition about whether he should marry a white woman or a black woman. Oberndorf and Freud haggled over the meaning of this dream for a couple of months until Freud just got fed up with Oberndorf's "resistances" and brought the analysis to an end. If one goes back through all of Freud's case histories, one finds a similar pattern of patients reporting how astonished they were at the seemingly arbitrary conclusions Freud reached, and how Freud stubbornly resisted objections to his own formulaic psychoanalytic interpretations. Of course, this was nothing new. The fiasco of Freud's seduction theory arose in the same manner [see Esterson 1993].

To provide another salient instance, the Wolf Man has described Freud's interpretation of his famous dream about wolves as "terribly far fetched" [in Obholzer 1982, 35]. He also complained that Freud insisted that he would one day remember the events that had made him ill, but he never did. Even more telling, the Wolf Man told Karin Obholzer that his dream was not about wolves at all, but about white dogs. It would not have sounded nearly so good for Freud to have called his famous patient the Dog Man, so he became the Wolf Man! This convenient transposition allowed Freud to bolster his dubious clinical analysis with arguments about wolves drawn from folklore.

Freud's case histories are littered with these kinds of discrepancies, which generally arise from an overzealous effort to make the facts fit the theory. Once one has collected and examined them all, and has fully realized how loose the inference generally is by which Freud goes from such clinical facts to speculative inferences, then to theory, one begins not only to question the whole undertaking but to repudiate it entirely. More often than not, Freud came up with interpretations that were astonishingly implausible, which his patients understandably did not accept and which sometimes involved blatant distortions of the facts.

All of this explains why Freud had so much trouble establishing a discipline in which disciples could ever come up with the same theoretically "correct" interpretations he did. His interpretations were sometimes so arbitrary that there was rarely any real consensus. As I have argued in my article about Freud's case histories, this is a significant part of the reason why Freud felt the need for privatizing psychoanalytic training. Given that his interpretations could neither be replicated nor proven, there was no other effective way of getting agreement with other psychoanalysts other than by institutionalizing a formal process by which "resistances" could be completely eliminated from the minds of psychoanalytic candidates. That process was the training analysis.

MB-J: If what you're saying is true, it would mean that Freud substituted an initiatory, cultlike process for the scientific mode of reproduction of knowledge. Would you go so far as to say that Freud, under the cover of elaborating a science of the psyche, in reality founded a new religion founded on the blind adhesion to several founding myths?

FS: Freud would have been shocked to hear this said about him, but I do think that psychoanalysis fulfills all the needs that religions used to fulfill and that it has also adopted some of religion's institutional features. Much of psychoanalysis's appeal is that it provides an answer to almost everything, and, in this respect, there is no modern scientific theory quite like it. It makes Darwinism, which certainly explains a lot about the world, look like a paltry and rather specialized philosophy. What can one really achieve by applying natural selection to one's own life and problems? Not much, at least on an individual psychological level, or at the level of incredible detail that Freud aspired to explain. Although much progress has been made in the field of Darwinian psychology, this approach to human behavior still cannot hold a candle to psychoanalysis in terms of its explanatory scope for individual behavior.

When one is in possession of a theory that explains just about everything, almost nothing is refutable anymore, and what one ends up with is more like a religion or a pseudoscience than a science. As I view it, psychoanalysis is just such a pseudoscience, and it cannot be denied that it also has all the properties of a religion. There is a wonderful article written in the 1970s by George Weisz [1975], dealing with the sectarian properties of psychoanalysis, and I don't think anybody has improved on that insightful analysis. Even Freud's own disciples, such as Hanns Sachs or Max Schur, talked openly about the sectlike qualities of the psychoanalytic community. By the way, it is not uncommon in the history of science to see people banding together in alliances of power, coordinating their responses to critics, founding new journals, and so on—especially in the incipient stages of a new theoretical discipline. But this kind of behavior, which one can clearly associate with sectarianism, rarely becomes the be-all and end-all of each new field's way of constructing knowledge. Psychoanalysis, on the contrary, never outgrew these sectarian tactics. The principal reason, as I have said, is because this churchlike construction of knowledge is the only real way to obtain clinical agreement among psychoanalysts. If the psychoanalytic community was not socially constructed, through the training analysis and the inherently unscientific frame of mind it inculcates, there would never be any real consensus at all.

In short, what is wrong with the discipline of psychoanalysis is not just the theories. False theories can always be discarded if the underlying methods are sound. The greatest failing of psychoanalysis is its blatant rejection of the scientific method. Without such methods for critical thinking, a discipline inevitably drifts from one pseudoscientific system of belief to another. That, in my opinion, is Freud's most tragic legacy.

5

Truth, Science, and the Failures of Psychoanalysis: Frederick Crews Reveals Why He Became a Freud Skeptic

Interviewed by Todd Dufresne

Frederick Crews was born in Philadelphia in 1933 and has spent most of his adult life in California. He received his bachelor of arts degree from Yale University and in 1955 began graduate studies in English at Princeton University. In 1958, PhD in hand, he joined the English faculty at the University of California, Berkeley, where he remained until his retirement in 1994.

His numerous books include *The Sins of the Fathers: Hawthorne's Psychological Themes* (1966), which established psychoanalytic literary criticism as an academic field; *Skeptical Engagements* (1986), which explained the grounds of his drastically altered view of Freudianism; and *The Critics Bear It Away* (1992), which won a PEN prize for the best American book of previously uncollected essays. Today Crews is probably best known for feature articles first published in 1993 and 1994 in *The New York Review of Books*, later collected as *The Memory Wars: Freud's Legacy in Dispute* (1995). These articles were decisive turning points in the popular reception of Freud and psychoanalysis. Crews has since become one of the most prominent faces of Freud criticism. His invaluable edited collection of seminal criticisms of psychoanalysis was published in 1998 as *Unauthorized Freud: Doubters Confront a Legend*. Finally, I should note that Crews is also widely known for his send-ups of contemporary literary criticism, *The Pooh Perplex* (1963) and *Postmodern Pooh* (2001).

I interviewed Crews in his Berkeley home on the morning of November 7, 1998, where he reflected on the making of a Freud skeptic.

. . .

TD: When did you become interested in psychoanalysis, and why?

FC: As a college undergraduate I was passionately interested in Nietzsche, who made up much of my recreational reading. I found his bold formulations exhilarating and liberating—so scornful of every prejudice and petty convention! When I eventually got around to Freud, his work struck me as a scientific rendering of everything I'd admired, but also found disturbingly volatile, in Nietzsche. As a graduate student I found myself reading Freud as an escape from my training in a narrow history-of-ideas historicism, which was no more fulfilling than the New Critical principles I had learned as an undergraduate at Yale. Neither approach struck me as doing justice to the psychological dynamism I was finding in great works of literature. Dabbling in Freud on the sly felt pleasantly subversive without actually entailing the slightest risk.

It was in this frame of mind that I became interested in Nathaniel Hawthorne, who seemed to me uncannily Freudian. Like Freud, Hawthorne was obsessed with sexual sin bearing incestuous overtones, with secret guilt, with internalization of the community's repressiveness, and with self-punishment of a masochistic kind. When Hawthorne wrote about his Puritan ancestors, he brilliantly depicted them as whipping half-naked adulteresses through the streets of Salem, thus gratifying their own hypocritically repressed prurience. Powerful stuff! My professors, along with the whole moralizing tradition of Eisenhower-era Hawthorne criticism, wanted to look the other way. And so I drew what seemed to me an unavoidable conclusion: Hawthorne's novels confirmed Freud's science.

Only later, after I had gone public with my psychoanalytic enthusiasm, did it occur to me that the Hawthorne-Freud kinship could be explained in historical rather than scientific terms. They were both Romantic thinkers—as, of course, was Nietzsche. All three were engaged in the same broad project of exploring the divided self and the cost that society exacts on erotic freedom. In short, Freud wasn't so much explaining Hawthorne as recapitulating his concerns in an unjustifiably deterministic idiom.

TD: In *The Critics Bear It Away,* you mention the perception in some quarters that your later work is self-destructive. And you grant that your turn away from psychoanalysis cost you your "personal fiefdom." Can you expand on these comments?

FC: From 1966 through 1970 I taught a graduate seminar at Berkeley in psychoanalytic criticism. The seminar was always fully enrolled, with lots of auditors cycling through. So a large number of people were watching what was going on. The brightest students in our graduate program attended, including many who had gone through psychotherapy. The students and I shared a sense that Freudian principles were giving us access to the motivational core of literature—invisible, of course, to everybody else. We kept experiencing what I now call the aha effect: moments of apparent recognition when the perceived data seem to fit the theory to perfection, as the classroom becomes flooded with a sense of self-satisfied, giddy awe. This was so exciting that we never paused to reflect on the fact that our aha insights were incompatible with one another.

If the heart of a given literary work was anality, then it could hardly be orality as well. But thanks to the glib laxity of psychoanalytic discourse, either version could be made utterly convincing for the moment. And, actually, this was part of the reason I got cold feet about psychoanalysis. It worked too well, seemed too easy. There had to be something wrong with ideas that arouse that much enthusiasm without leading to any final clarity or resolution. If psychoanalysis lent itself to so many contradictory avenues of interpretation, all of which seemed to be emotionally confirmed during discussion, then maybe there was something wrong with the idea of emotional confirmation. The whole business eventually struck me as rather cheap and coercive.

TD: Why did it take you so long to break with psychoanalytic ideas?

FC: Human frailty! I was gripped by embarrassment, chagrin, and hope that I would turn out to have been right after all. Freud himself went through a similar phase of indecisiveness in the later 1890s. When he famously "abandoned the seduction theory," he didn't actually renounce it, even though medical ethics obliged him to advise his colleagues that his published findings—and cures—were spurious. His letters during the following year or two show that he was still hoping to be bailed out by cures. The need to avoid humiliation took precedence over any sense of public responsibility. Similarly, I had published works of literary criticism and theoretical statements that were adamant and more than a little disdainful toward nonbelievers in Freudian truth. And now I found myself starting to agree, privately, with the people I'd characterized as lacking in psychological insight. What was I going to do about having painted myself into such a corner? Well, any imaginable course of action looked mortifying, and so, like Freud, I just keep postponing an ultimate reckoning.

TD: Did your political views ever affect your growing skepticism about psychoanalysis in the 1960s?

FC: That's a good question, but it's not easy to answer. I was already a Freudian when, on leave at the Center for Advanced Study in the Behavioral Sciences in 1965–1966, I joined some Stanford faculty members in learning as much as we could about Indochina. The Vietnam War looked to us like a disaster from any point of view you could name. When I returned to Berkeley, I worked with like-minded colleagues on the Faculty Peace Committee, and shortly thereafter I became its cochair. We organized demonstrations and made speeches at high schools, clubs, churches—wherever we could get a foot in the door. But public opinion was largely against us, and the atmosphere was quite tense for a while. My activism subsided around 1970, when even Republicans were turning against the war. It's certainly arresting to ponder the fact that I was breaking with Freud in that same period. But just as there were objective political developments that made it unnecessary for me to keep agitating against the war, so there were intellectual considerations behind my disaffection from Freud. I don't much care for the assumption that deep psychological factors must be the "real" explanation for such changes.

TD: What, in your opinion, are the core propositions of psychoanalysis, and what's wrong with them?

FC: In one sense, there are *no* core propositions—that is, nothing that a given analyst wouldn't jettison in a pinch. Psychoanalysis was replete with ambiguities and self-contradictions from the very outset, and as it splintered into various rival orthodoxies and began coping with objections by half incorporating them into its doctrine, the confusion got steadily worse. Today, analysts have little in common with one another, or with Freud, beyond a certain pose of deep knowingness and a determination to stay in business at all cost.

TD: But given that caveat, there are a number of ideas associated with Freud that have enduring power in public consciousness.

FC: For Freud, the core of psychoanalysis was the idea that adult psychoneuroses are brought about by the repression of early sexual wishes that trigger a terror of punishment. Since scarcely anyone, including the analysts, believes that dogma anymore, there would be no point in my refuting it here. But a handful of Freud's innovations have had real staying power. I'll review the four notions that come closest to being shared by practitioners today.

1. *Repression*, which can be invoked without reference to Freud's obviously erroneous, echt-Victorian model of pathogenesis through mortification over sex. To be sure, some analysts—those who don't care for the male-centered Oedipus complex and who want psychoanalysis to join forces with the recovered-memory movement—prefer to replace repression with Pierre Janet's idea of dissociation, which Freud, in fact, plagiarized and slightly altered when announcing his own favorite concept. The difference between the two notions, though inconspicuous, turns out to be operationally important, since dissociation encourages the analyst to finger "perpetrators" of trauma-inducing deeds, whereas repression is typically a matter of self-generated harm. What repression and dissociation have in common, though, is the idea that symptomatic behavior can be caused by the blocking out of a memory, resulting in unconscious disruption of the psyche for ensuing decades.

Without some such tenet, however watered down, analysts would have no justification for doing what they like to do best—namely, showing patients, over an expensively protracted course of treatment, how their dream reports, behavioral quirks, free associations, and slips of the tongue fall into patterns that cohere along theoretically favored lines. Thus, by seeming to demonstrate that the patient's self-conception is superficial and in need of a painstaking makeover, the invoking of repression-dissociation establishes the analyst as the hermeneutically superior party.

Likewise, an academic Freudian needs to invoke some version of repression in order to underwrite his claim to be disclosing the secret meaning of cultural products or of historical developments. Repression legitimates the reflexive dismissal of what seems to other observers—fellow scholars or the clueless public—to be patently "there." Then the way is clear for a wanton application of theoretically predetermined moves. To put it bluntly, the chief academic function of repression in our time is to facilitate tenure-conducive logorrhea, which will have the desired effect so long as the already tenured evaluators of the submitted discourse still regard "psychoanalytic knowledge" as something other than an oxymoron.

2. *The unconscious,* which is a reification of the idea that, under the sway of repression or dissociation, the mind becomes enduringly divided against itself. Perhaps we do, after all, have a true universal here: all proponents of analytic theory believe that intrapsychic conflict is structurally ordered in a way that seals off certain material from awareness. But when we ask them just what the unconscious contains and how it works, we once again come face-to-face with chaos. There is no appreciable convergence of views.

Characterized so variously, the unconscious can't be regarded as a detected mental agency featuring such and such well-established properties. Rather, it is a personification of those explanatory factors to which the analyst is favorably inclined on a priori grounds. Otherwise stated, the unconscious is a place marker for all the ways in which the analyst, according to his particular school of thought, will negate and redirect the patient's self-perception. When a Freudian says, "We must listen carefully to what the unconscious is trying to tell us," what he means is, "I intend to keep insisting on the same old 'deep' banalities."

Please note that the Freudian unconscious is not the same thing as the loosely named "cognitive unconscious," a term meant to honor the indisputable fact that much of our brain activity occurs beyond our notice. Psychoanalytic sophists often try to adopt the protective coloration afforded by research into such phenomena as subliminal perception and automated routines that were once mastered through conscious effort. But there is no overlap between such nonconscious activity and the Freudian "psychodynamic" unconscious, which behaves like a whole second mind that resembles the first one except for its troll-like obstreperousness and secretiveness. It perceives, thinks, and remembers; it schemes; it makes demands; it generates symbols; and, when scrutinized by Freud, it engages in clever and diagnostically revealing multilingual puns. But for other analysts it will do quite different stunts, because, as I said, it's really just a concretization of their interpretative bias.

3. *Free association.* Virtually all psychoanalysts encourage their patients to issue an apparently random sequence of utterances, usually after a topical prompt of some kind, and a dialogue follows in which the analyst seizes on telltale phrases, asks for further associations, and gradually zooms in

on an alleged unconscious preoccupation that has supposedly been determining the whole stream. Freud saw this as an enormously powerful and reliable tool for stripping away defenses and unearthing the patient's traumatic early history. What a staggering claim—as if we could get from the couch straight back to the nursery without having to worry about the millions of experiential variables lying between the two!

That confidence has largely dropped away, but analysts still believe they can learn things about "the unconscious" through the probing of associations. As usual, though, they are self-deceived. Everything about free association is epistemically contaminated, from the coaxing and coaching that gradually "Freudianize" the patient's thoughts, through the therapist's option to skip past all associations that don't fit his theory, to the confirmatory bias that keeps both parties uncognizant of rival ways in which a given phrase might be considered meaningful. The whole process is about as free as a game of Twenty Questions, but it's considerably less honest, because the patient is given the impression that a real inquiry is taking place.

4. *Transference,* or the idea that the patient's behavior toward the analyst is a reenactment of early relationships. Once again, Freud held this doctrine in a graphically sexual form that is now generally forgotten. But the milder modern version still serves the general function that it did for Freud when he introduced it in his Dora case—namely, as a means of sparing the analyst from responsibility for any seductive and/or annoying conduct toward the patient. Freud began appealing to transference when his patients rejected his wild interpretations; if they disagreed with him, he decided, it could only be because he must have been serving as a stand-in for an ambivalently regarded parent. And transference loomed ever larger in his theory as an excuse for his record of consistent therapeutic failure. What could even the greatest of psychoanalysts accomplish in the face of this compulsion to repeat infantile entanglements?

There are three outstanding flaws in every version of transference that has come to my attention. The first, as I've indicated, is that recourse to this idea exacerbates the inequality between therapist and patient. The second is that, if taken seriously, transference disqualifies the knowledge claims that are supposedly validated by the patient's eventual self-insight; if the analyst really does serve as a parent surrogate, that fact in itself would suffice to explain why the patient will eventually bow to his will. And finally, even when transference is stripped of all meaning except "the patient's emotional involvement with the therapist," it still remains unclear why patients *ought* to get sucked into such a dependent intimacy.

Analytic theory has dealt extensively with the thorny problem of bringing the transference to a satisfactory conclusion—apparently a chancy outcome. But if psychoanalysis were as humane as it purports to be, surely its literature would feature a debate over the wisdom of attaching patients to this tar baby in the first place. No such debate has occurred, because psychoanalysis *is* transference in this minimalist but still very questionable sense. As soon as the patient is treated as an equal, competent to think rationally about his or her objective situation, we are standing outside the whole psychoanalytic framework.

Incidentally, matters are made worse, not better, when the increasingly fashionable notion of *countertransference* is added to the mix. If each party is using the other as an unconscious pawn, both are being emotionally exploited. And, of course, the recovery of "truth" is no longer remotely feasible, since neither party is primarily devoted to it, even in theory. Without either knowledge or cure in view, and with a bumpy emotional road ahead, the only remaining question is: why bother?

TD: So what do you consider to be the most fatal flaw of psychoanalysis?

FC: Its epistemic nullity. When you generate "knowledge" in a private setting through manifestly suggestive procedures, applying hermeneutic "rules" that amount to the sheerest license; when you report your uncheckable findings in self-servingly anecdotal form; and when you then reply to criticism by declaring the critics to be unconsciously troubled, as witnessed by their inability to agree with you, you have fashioned something that's the very opposite of an authentic investigative instrument.

This should be kept in mind when the analysts tell us about the "progress" they've made since Freud's day. We can all be grateful that penis envy and the death instinct are in retreat, but on what basis should we lend credence to the innovations that are replacing them? So far as I can tell, psychoanalytic methodology is just as primitive today as it was in 1900.

TD: John Horgan, in *Scientific American*, wrote a piece in 1996 in which he claimed that Freud was still alive and well in therapeutic circles. What is the lasting value, if any, of Freudian psychoanalysis or its derivatives?

FC: I know Horgan and have discussed psychoanalytic issues with him in person and by e-mail. He has just published a book, *The Undiscovered Mind* [1999], and I've read and criticized a draft chapter of it that deals with me. The idea that Freud won't go away gratifies Horgan for reasons that I find strange. It isn't that he actually believes anything Freud asserted, but Freud, he thinks, deserves credit for having posed the big questions that are ducked by academic psychology. To my mind, this is just an extension of the religion-based animus against empiricism that was on view in Horgan's *The End of Science*. If the chapter of the new book that I saw is typical, I'm afraid he has written about psychoanalysis without a broad acquaintance with its literature or any appreciation of its power to cause social harm.

The short answer to your question is that, in my opinion, psycho-analysis belongs on the rubbish heap. Which is not to say that we shouldn't study it as a historical phenomenon and cultural influence. But it has proved considerably worse than useless as accurate psychological lore, as a research paradigm, and as a guide to sound principles of treatment. If much of the twentieth century has indeed belonged to Freud, then we lost about seventy years worth of potential gains in knowledge while befuddling ourselves with an essentially medieval conception of the "possessed" mind.

TD: Freud began as a scientist and had established a career as a neu-rologist. What caused him to abandon the standards of science in his train-ing and turn to what we would call pseudoscience?

FC: A full answer would require about a hundred pages, but I'll pro-vide an outline here. First, Freud's biographers agree that he was intently ambitious to become known as a great scientific pioneer and that he was increasingly frustrated and infuriated by the denial of his application for a professorship, which he would eventually secure through soliciting the bribery of a state official. He was also desperate to make money for his fam-ily's sake, but his therapeutic practice was shrinking drastically in the later 1890s. These were all inducements to premature enthusiasm about cure-all notions—first his seduction theory and then psychoanalysis proper—that he should have approached more warily. And already by *Studies on Hyste-ria* in 1895, he had begun his lifelong practice of fibbing about therapeu-tic outcomes. That's not pseudoscience but flat-out scientific and medical fraud. But, of course, pseudoscience and fraud go hand in hand, because the faked results are needed to shore up a theory that doesn't work.

As for Freud's abandonment of neurology, back in the 1880s he had acquired a fateful affinity for the discredited Mesmeric tradition, of which psychoanalysis would prove to be the most popular modern example. This change of orientation began taking shape when he apprenticed himself intellectually to Jean-Martin Charcot, who was reviving hypnosis as a tool for delving—very naively—into the psyches of alleged hysterics. Although Freud was also well acquainted with Charcot's great rival Hippolyte Bernheim, who understood that hypnosis was epistemically unreliable because it operates through suggestion, he chose to believe Charcot, not Bernheim, on this cardinal point.

The whole psychoanalytic house of cards was erected on that initial blunder. Although Freud gave up employing hypnosis per se in his ventriloquizing approach to patients, he continued to badger them for concurrence with his pet ideas, all the while retaining a Charcot-like indifference to the overwhelming problem of suggestion as a pollutant of his "findings." *This* is the respect in which Freud strayed the farthest from his sound training in neurology. As Frank Sulloway has shown, he remained a cryptic "biologist of the mind," but methodologically, he had become a perfect crackpot, with no more empirical prudence than Swedenborg or Velikovsky or Deepak Chopra.

After Freud failed to win glory in the 1880s through his ill-advised promotion of cocaine as a panacea, and as he and his madcap friend Wilhelm Fliess began engaging in cocaine-fueled flights of neo-Darwinian speculation about the human organism and its instinctual drives, mainstream inductive science appeared more and more contemptible to him. He wanted to make one grand Promethean leap into greatness—one that would settle the hash not just of scientific conformists but also of the whole oppressive Christian order, whose hypocrisies and prejudices were so understandably galling to him. As the Virgilian epigraph to *The Interpretation of Dreams*, with its reference to stirring up hell, might suggest to you, psychoanalysis was meant as a revolutionary countertheological undertaking. And, after all, that's just what it succeeded in becoming—a transvaluation of values in which the Catholic hierarchy of reason and virtue over sex and aggression was put to rout. By 1900, scientific determinism was little more than the fig leaf with which Freud covered a project whose motivation was fully Nietzschean in spirit.

Here, by the way, I'm giving you a thumbnail sketch of Freud that doesn't match the goody-goody bourgeois figure depicted by guardians of institutional psychoanalysis, such as Ernest Jones and Peter Gay. We've been living all these years with a Freud who has had to serve as the confidence-inspiring logo of a prosperous guild. With the release of many classified manuscript materials over the coming decade, I think you'll see that Freud was more of a daredevil than the analytic faithful could ever admit. The real Freud was a passionate and impulsive fellow, if also quite wacky and utterly scornful of the weak and the sick who were supposed to have benefited from his ministrations. But he couldn't come up to Nietzsche's standard of courage as a foe of the moral order. He finally chose to bask in the aura of kindly sagacity that the innocent, god-hungry public bestowed on him.

TD: Why haven't partisans of psychoanalysis been able to read the writing on the wall?

FC: Freud, you must understand, was a master rhetorician who could lull just about anyone into taking his word that he'd really made the careful observations and effected the wonderful cures that he describes. His self-portrait as a martyr and hero is absolutely brilliant as well as absolutely false. And he provides us with the thrill of making everything explainable in terms of his system—something that an authentic scientist would never try to do. People who read Freud and only Freud are going to be hooked by this spellbinding fairy tale. There's no mystery, then, to the tenacity with which Freudians, especially "well-analyzed" Freudians, cling to the faith. Psychoanalysis is a religion, and religions turn all perceived facts to their own purposes. In the Middle Ages, the fathers of the church developed a way of immunizing their intellectual experience against surprises by construing everything in the Old Testament, along with everything in the physical universe, as an illustration of revealed Christian truth. This is also the cozy style of psychoanalysis; all facts are Freudian to the Freudian eye. That's what I meant by saying that the psychoanalytic tradition is anti-empirical to its core.

TD: What are the intellectual and psychological tricks by which Freud seduces his readers into abandoning critical thought and accepting his theories?

FC: I'll single out three of them. One is his superbly timed knack of anticipating objections, appearing to accede to them with charming flashes of false modesty, and then steaming blithely past them a few pages or paragraphs later. Freud concedes nothing, all the while leaving us with the impression that he has bent over backwards to accommodate our doubts.

Second, there's the father-knows-best stratagem, which fits beautifully with pseudohospitality to objections. Freud's most standard move is an appeal to the uniqueness of the psychoanalyst's access to the secrets of the unconscious. You may well doubt, he says, that little boys want to fornicate with their mothers and murder their fathers, or that paranoia results from repressed homosexuality, or that music is sublimated farting, but if only you heard what our patients reveal to us under the special conditions of our therapy, your misgivings would vanish. That appeal, though intellectually shabby, is powerful, because we *want* to put ourselves under the care of authorities who have already ascertained the big important truths about our condition. There's even a certain swooning thrill involved in surrendering to propositions that contradict everyday experience: *credo quia absurdum est.*

Finally, Freud is a master storyteller who manipulates suspense in a way that makes us his accomplices in bringing things to satisfactory closure. The closure simply amounts to his application of a priori dogmas to the puzzle at hand, but it doesn't feel that way; we get the same satisfaction that attends the denouement of a well-crafted murder mystery. Not surprisingly, Freud was an avid reader of Arthur Conan Doyle. His case histories are cast in the same mold, with you-know-who playing the role of the infallible Holmes.

TD: In your edited collection, *Unauthorized Freud,* you speak of the dangers of overkill and then go on to describe Freud as a bumbling "Inspector Clouseau" and an "intellectual megalomaniac." You also state that Freud is "the most overrated figure in the entire history of science." Isn't there a danger that critics like yourself, who are already marginalized for their views, will be further marginalized by such candor and a flair for controversy?

FC: Of course there is—and reviews of my book show this. People quote these phrases and say, "This is intemperate, irrational, over the top." But that's because they assume that Freud, for all his faults, must after all have been the great discoverer he claimed to be. Well, he just wasn't. If psychoanalysis is a self-validating knowledge machine, as Popper, Grünbaum, Cioffi, and Macmillan, among others, have shown it to be, and if it nevertheless has enjoyed an enormous vogue through the greater part of [the twentieth] century, who could rival Freud as the world's most overrated scientist? On the question of intellectual megalomania, you need only draw up a list of the phenomena that Freud thought he was explaining—from cell division to death, from the prehistoric origins of guilt to the meaning of art and music and dreams—and you'll see that he was indeed the most ambitious scientific thinker ever to be taken seriously. Who even comes close as a rival for self-importance? As for Peter Sellers's Inspector Clouseau, the detailed critical accounts of Freud's case histories that I put together in *Unauthorized Freud* reveal a level of obtuse bumbling on Freud's part that's scarcely matched by anything to be found in *The Pink Panther*. He couldn't even distinguish between his own weird fantasies and those he purported to extract from his patients' minds!

TD: Do you consider yourself an extremist? Are hard-core skeptics, by definition, extremists?

FC: I've never met anyone who regards himself as an extremist. Extremism, in any case, is not an applicable category when it comes to evaluating ideas. It's meaningful only in the context of policy. An extremist, for example, would be someone who advocates a first-strike nuclear attack on a cold war antagonist or who calls for euthanizing the retarded. If you find a given system of thought to be *extremely* off base, and if that's what it is, you've simply done your job correctly. On the other hand, if you've failed to note some positive features, then to that extent you're just wrong, not extremist.

Most people believe that, on any given issue, "the truth lies somewhere between" poles x and y, and on that basis they automatically apply such labels as extremist to those of us who maintain that a well-regarded fad was founded entirely on mistakes and falsehoods. The skeptical vocation requires pursuing truth wherever it appears to lead, without shrinking from the consequences.

So if by "hard-core skepticism" you mean what I called "strong skepticism," I perceive it as consistent, not extreme. Many of the claims made by our revered religious traditions—that people get repeatedly reincarnated; that God wrote out his favorite precepts on a couple of tablets and presented them to a guy on a mountain; that somebody rose from his grave and flew up into the clouds, where he still resides; that illness and death are just illusions; and so forth—are naturalistic, not mystical, assertions. A strong skeptic regards them as fair game, and why not?

TD: But what about competing notions of truth, say, between the African Azande and Western views on witchcraft?

FC: We've done some amazing things in the twentieth century. We've discovered to some degree of precision the structure of elemental matter. We've sent rockets outside the solar system with a tolerance of a few miles in one direction or the other. We've made medical discoveries that have been validated by the results they've produced. In many ways we've shown that the mathematical, experimental paradigm of science works. Thus, we have every right to be confident that the Western way is absolutely better, for bringing the world within the range of human understanding, than beating on tom-toms and pushing pins into dolls. One can appreciate why many people find science too impersonal and unpoetical for their taste. But when they go on to revise it so as to suit their politics, great social mischief can result. Just think about our recovered-memory fiasco, about which I've written at some length. It wouldn't have occurred if great numbers of therapists, patients, and judges and jurors hadn't taken at face value Freud's creaky notions about the self-divided mind and its pristinely retrievable secrets.

TD: Given your literary background, why do you have this lifelong interest in the norms of reason and empiricism?

FC: I never cease marveling at this question, which I'm frequently asked. How could anyone who cares about knowledge in any field *not* be committed to those norms? The question, I would say, rests on a faulty premise, confusing the subjective state in which literature is produced with an anything-goes approach to statements *about* the field. I can only protest that there's nothing inherently antiempirical about literary subject matter or, indeed, any other subject matter. To handle literary-critical issues with cogency, you have to be committed to the weighing of evidence, the testing of hypotheses, the entertaining of rival explanations. It's just the coin of the realm—or it was, anyway, before the extreme antifoundationalism of poststructuralism came along.

TD: Would you explain what you mean by "extreme antifoundationalism"?

FC: Certainly. Ever since Thomas Kuhn's *The Structure of Scientific Revolutions* in 1962, it's been widely conceded that large-scale theories, or paradigms, don't just go away when inconsistent evidence begins to turn up. In the absence of a clearly better paradigm, it's reasonable to try tweaking the old one to make room for the newly found anomalies. It's also generally recognized by now that there's no algorithm for the scientific method—that is, there's no way of being assuredly right in one's propositions simply by virtue of adhering to a set of impeccable methodological rules. We will all have to do without foundations of knowledge in this a priori sense. The key remaining question, however, is whether this awakening from the positivist dream means that the choice among theories is strictly a matter of social power and ideological convenience. Kuhn rather plaintively denied that this was the import of his work, but poststructuralists within the humanities have been eager to understand him in exactly that spirit. They are extreme antifoundationalists because they generalize Kuhn's paradigm crises into a sweeping denigration of science as just another "discourse" that's totally at the mercy of hegemonic prejudice. Now *all* evidential constraints on theory are dismissed as trivial, and evidence itself is stigmatized as a retrograde notion. In short, we see a nihilistic posture toward any and all grounds of objective judgment.

TD: Where does deconstruction fit into this picture?

FC: Deconstruction was a particular dogma about the self-canceling or self-ironizing character of language. Its "finding"—the same result in every single case!—was that text A, B, or C couldn't help but undermine itself, because that's just given in the way that words structurally entail their opposites. As you know, after a few years this critical exercise became a bore even to its practitioners. Unfortunately, though, what the humanists found tiresome about deconstruction wasn't its central flaw, namely, its epistemic circularity. Rather, they decided that linguistic determinism was too remote from the agenda of the left; it didn't have a proper political tone.

Thus, in the 1990s, we've seen literary study balkanized into a number of engaged "discourses"—feminist, ethnic, lesbian and gay—that don't even pay lip service to the old ideal of explaining what's "there" in the text. Now it's simply "what's there *for us*." From this position, which the old Marxists used to call revolutionary subordination, major consequences flow—not the least of which is that a scholar's fast and loose way with evidence can no longer weigh heavily against his or her academic appointment or promotion. What's taught in graduate school is precisely how to rig the game of interpretation in favor of one's chosen doctrine, and a prestige-conscious department will be hoping not to hire the best scholars but to give wide representation to the current "isms." Thus, it's positively unhealthy, professionally speaking, to be weighted down with scruples about self-validating and question-begging means of reaching conclusions.

If, by the way, you dare to wax nostalgic for the days when empirical criteria did matter academically, you'll surely be branded antigay, antifemale, racist, and so forth. Professors are well aware of this sword of Damocles hanging over them, though hardly anyone mentions it. Academic humanists have never been noted for their bravery, but the penalty for defending objectivity has now become too scary for all but a few curmudgeons or retirees to risk incurring.

TD: With your current view of academic politics, would you want to enter literary studies if you were starting over today?

FC: Certainly not. But the question is moot because, with my "positionality" as a straight white male, my distaste for identity politics, and my explicit commitment to Enlightenment values, I'd never be offered a job in today's academic marketplace. There's no demand for my "ism" anymore, namely, empiricism.

TD: One of your books is called *Skeptical Engagements*. Could you characterize your relation to skepticism as an intellectual attitude?

FC: Let's distinguish here between weak and strong skepticism. By weak skepticism I mean a commitment to taking as little as possible for granted, and relying on logic, not authority, when addressing issues. A strong skeptic applies this orientation to all problems instead of backing off in deference to the mysteries of "religious truth." Well, you can put me down as a skeptic in both senses. But, in practice, I've kept my dim view of religion pretty much to myself. In doing so, I think I've been able to reach a wider audience for my critiques of methodological follies. I've always felt that ordinary weak skepticism is applicable to the high-level theoretical issues that get debated within the humanities and social sciences. I've tried to make this point repeatedly in my publications.

I'll give you just one example. My ex-colleagues are baffled as to why I would stoop to writing an essay about the patent nonsense of UFO abduction, as I did in 1998. What that essay shows, however, is that the postmodern intellectuals who scoff at empirical standards arrive at the same stupidity—the same inability to draw a line against obvious delusion—as the most ignorant dupes of "abduction" therapists. For fear of being thought complicit with NASA, capitalism, and Western rationality, the trendy academics have to claim that they possess no means of deciding whether or not abduction reports are true. That's colossally funny, I'd say, as a confession of intellectual bankruptcy. I enjoy showing how the common sense of ordinary people is superior to such apparent sophistication.

And let me put in one final word about Freud in this connection. With his various stratagems for deflecting attention from the scientific emptiness of his claims, he was very much a stage magician and mentalist. If, as a good working skeptic, you can detect the fallaciousness of astrology, channeling, and tarot reading, you have all the equipment needed to see through Freud. And I'm convinced that the future course of Freud studies lies precisely here, in exposing how he extracted cards from his sleeve and gave the appearance of sawing the mind in half and producing it whole again. There's a good deal of amusement, as well as edification, to be had through such inquiry. I won't be conducting it myself, but I hope to have sketched some outlines as to how it might proceed.

TD: What do skeptics need to do to elevate the skeptical movement to the forefront of culture and thought?

FC: I'm afraid that, at my age, I'm a bit more jaded than you are! Skepticism isn't going to occupy the forefront of thought, because humankind, in its all-out flight from the prospect of personal extinction, loves to delude itself in any number of ways. That's just what *Homo sapiens* is like, with some happy exceptions that will never amount to a majority. You are doing yeoman service in stemming the tide of irrationality, but most of our fellow citizens regard the skeptical habit of mind as blasphemous. We can pop certain balloons—exposing a faith healer, explaining a UFO report—but people will still demand miracles and divine visitations, and they'll keep showering their hard-won savings on the mountebanks who market such trash.

At most, skeptics can work to improve educational standards, so that, for example, a young person wouldn't be able to graduate from college without having had some exposure to objective criteria for judging the merits of ideas. But even that goal looks rather utopian, given the present state of higher learning.

Let me anticipate your next question. If skepticism isn't going to prevail, why do I persist in deploying it? The answer is, because it's fun! I want to exercise my brain, like the rest of my organism, to the fullest extent while it's still in working order. If, as I hope, such exercise produces some useful social effects, so much the better. But I'm going to continue being a skeptic, in any case, because any other relationship to ideas would feel phony to me.

TD: Do you feel that you have written enough about Freud and that it's time to move on?

FC: Absolutely. After almost twenty years of explaining and illustrating the same basic critique, I will just refer interested parties to *Skeptical Engagements*, *The Memory Wars*, and *Unauthorized Freud*. Anyone who is unmoved by my reasoning there isn't going to be touched by anything further I might try to say.

6

Freud and Interpretation:
Frank Cioffi and Allen Esterson
Discuss Freud's Legacy

Interviewed by Todd Dufresne

Frank Cioffi was born in New York in 1928 but received his universi-ty education in England. He has taught at the National University of Sin-gapore; University of Kent at Canterbury; University of California, Berke-ley; and University of Essex. He is the author of *Wittgenstein on Freud and Frazer* (1998) and *Freud and the Question of Pseudoscience* (1998a). This sec-ond book collects together his best essays on Freud published since the ear-ly 1970s. He holds the honorary chair in philosophy at the University of Kent at Canterbury. Cioffi is venerated among professional Freud scholars, not just for his humor and tenacity concerning Freud and psychoanalysis but for his deep understanding of Freud's texts. Today he is considered a world expert on Freud's seduction theory, which has proven immensely influential among critics.

Allen Esterson studied physics at University College London and lec-tured in mathematics and physics at colleges of further education in Lon-don until his retirement in 1994. He is the author of a highly regarded book, *Seductive Mirage: An Exploration of the Work of Sigmund Freud* (1993), that examines Freud's case studies and his general expositions of psychoanaly-sis. In this book Esterson convincingly demonstrates that Freud's writings cannot be trusted. Esterson has also published several articles on Freud and psychoanalysis; these articles have appeared in such notable journals as *History of the Human Sciences, History of Psychiatry,* and *History of Psychology.* He wrote the entries for *"fantasy"* and *"seduction"* in the influential *The Freud Encyclopedia: Theory, Therapy, and Culture* (2002).

The interview took place on a park bench in Russell Square, London, on June 14, 2002, and was updated by the participants in August and September 2005. Cioffi and I also conducted a follow-up interview by e-mail in August 2005, which is included here as an addendum to the original interview.

. . .

TD: Allen, how did a trained physicist ever get involved with psychoanalysis?

AE: Entirely by accident! Arising from a passing remark, a cousin of mine suggested I should read Freud. I had glanced through some pages of *The Interpretation of Dreams* when I was much younger, and read more general writings about Freud at various times, but had never seriously examined any of his publications. As it happened, the only relevant book on the shelves of my local library was Muriel Gardiner's *The Wolf-Man and Sigmund Freud,* which contains the Wolf-Man case history and memoirs of the patient written late in life. Astonishment at the extraordinary nature of Freud's interpretations, recognition of his rhetorical gambits, and, in relation to one major item, suspicion that he was engaged in something close to fraudulent deception led to my writing a five-chapter critique of the case history. At the same time I was reading more widely—Clark's biography, Ellenberger's *The Discovery of the Unconscious,* and Sulloway's *Freud: Biologist of the Mind.* Finally, after reading Thornton's skeptical examination of the seduction theory papers in *Freud and Cocaine,* I consulted the original papers and compared them with his later accounts. The discrepancies between the several accounts, many of which, as I later discovered, Frank had already drawn attention to, led to my decision to write a book.

TD: Similarly, Frank, why would an analytic philosopher like yourself, someone who trained with A. J. Ayer no less, ever bother with psychoanalysis?

Frank Cioffi: Let me first explain how accidentally I came into Freud studies and then how it affected my view of analytic philosophy. I was recovering from dengue fever—this was in Singapore—and a kind friend put me up in a spare room in his home. Well, there were very few books in the bookcase, but among them were the first three volumes of the *Collected Papers* [of Freud]—which I read through for the first time. At Oxford I had to prepare for a compulsory abnormal psychology paper, but nothing I had heard from my lecturers—Oliver Zangwill and Brian Farrell—prepared me for what I found in the collected papers. In the idiom of the subculture from which I have only slowly emancipated myself, I thought, "What bullshit!" Only later did I discover that to deride Freud's status as the Columbus of the mental sciences was to brand oneself an eccentric. To my great astonishment, among the most vociferous of Freud's advocates were philosophers in the analytic tradition.

The result of my exposure to Oxford philosophy was that I became convinced that no one who familiarized himself with the problem of induction, the naturalistic fallacy, the distinction between analytic and synthetic truths, et cetera, could fail to become permanently immunized against fraudulent claims to knowledge. When I realized how many analytic philosophers were incapable of taking up a genuinely critical attitude towards Freud's pretension, I had to rethink my position concerning its educational value. Ironically, I drew a quasi-Freudian moral: the sources of conviction were not predominantly intellectual but affective, and so the logical astuteness of analytic philosophers was of little help to them.

TD: Did you still think that analytic philosophy could play a role in Freud studies?

FC: I thought it could play a very traditional role. Given any thesis, particularly one which generates controversy, try to clarify it by saying what kind of evidence could count for and against it. I was dissatisfied with the way the question of whether psychoanalysis was a pseudoscience was approached by many philosophers. For in their attempt to characterize pseudoscience, they fell into what might be called formalism—the notion that the dispute was a logical one over whether or not characteristic theses of psychoanalysis did or did not have observable implications. I had an intuition that this was not what was at issue.

From many hours spent in the basement of the Royal Society of Medicine library, I was surprised to discover that the traditional view about Freud's reception was false. There was just as much gratitude, even rapture, as there was hostility. But the main effect of my reading was to reinforce my conviction that those who construed the attacks on Freud's genuinely empirical status as focusing predominantly on the formal untestability of his theses were just wrong historically. The charge against Freud and his followers was that of dogmatism and tendentiousness, and these are much wider notions than untestability.

TD: In retrospect, have either of you made any mistakes in your reading of Freud and psychoanalysis?

FC: The great mistake that I made, in the first fifteen or twenty years of my dealing with Freud, was that I was overinfluenced by Karl Popper and his notion of testability. It's complicated to say why I went off testability, but I can simply say now that it isn't the open sesame that I once believed. Among the many reasons is this: if you look at the formulations that people embrace, when they give you an account of why they think Freud made such a great contribution to human understanding, you will find that it's impossible to say that they are untestable. They're not clear enough to be untestable. They are really mantras, things that people repeat and get satisfaction out of repeating, because it makes them think they have their finger on something deep in human life. Consider the statement that illness is something that people do, not something that happens to them. Analytic philosophers have disgraced themselves in the way they have repeated this remark. If you stop and ask them a very simple question—in what sense is a depression something that people do?—the question has never occurred to them. It's not that they don't have an adequate answer. It's that the thought has never occurred to them that these mantras, which they keep wheeling out from time to time when they are in a celebratory mood, have to be translated so that we know what they're actually saying. In what sense is an illness like depression something that a person is doing?

TD: And you, Allen? Any missteps?

AE: Yes, I can think of a couple of instances from *Seductive Mirage*. As a result of the way my first draft originated, I had started with the seduction theory episode. At a late stage, after my submitted draft had been accepted by Open Court in 1991, I realized I needed to lead up to that episode with a chapter on the earlier *Studies on Hysteria* that Freud wrote with Breuer. Largely because at that time I was not very familiar with the literature on Freud, I mistakenly regarded the contents of this volume as of lesser importance than the writings that followed. This was a serious error of judgment on my part, resulting in a pretty superficial survey of *Studies* that does not begin to do justice to its importance in a study of Freud's work. I think that is easily the weakest chapter in the book, and the only one I almost feel inclined to disown!

The only other mistake of any consequence is a section in one chapter in which I argue for the possibility that a short case history ["A Case of Paranoia Running Counter to the Psychoanalytic Theory of the Disease" (1915)] was fabricated. I was familiar with the fact that Freud had practiced a subterfuge in his 1899 "Screen Memories" paper, in which his supposed interlocutor was actually himself. And, of course, Peter Swales has demonstrated beyond reasonable doubt that the "acquaintance" in the famous *aliquis* analysis in *The Psychopathology of Everyday Life* is again Freud himself. There were some passages in the 1915 paper that aroused my suspicion that it was not authentic, and I spelled out my suspicions in *Seductive Mirage*. But, as was pointed out to me in person by Anthony Stadlen, there is a sentence in a letter from Freud to Abraham that indicates that the case was authentic. In addition, one of the points I made—supposedly in favor of my thesis—was not only mistaken, it was slipshod. Details of this are in an acknowledgement-of-error note I added to one of my postings on the Freud's Seduction Theory website—hosted by www.human-nature.com— which has an abridged version of my article "Jeffrey Masson and Freud's Seduction Theory" [1998], published in *History of the Human Sciences*.

Nevertheless, there is much that is dubious in that short case history, so I by no means wish to disown the whole section. And familiarity with the paper enabled me to recognize as fallacious one of Grünbaum's items of evidence in *The Foundations of Psychoanalysis*, purportedly showing that Freud was, at least on occasion, hospitable to refutations of his theories. He cites the very title of this paper as Freud's acknowledging the falsifiability of one of his theses. But, as my analysis shows, this is the opposite to the conclusion Grünbaum should have drawn from this particular paper, for it actually demonstrates that even when the evidence points to a refutation, Freud was able to use his elastic interpretative methodology to purportedly prove that this is not the case and that his theory was vindicated.

TD: Frank, in 1973, you delivered your now-famous BBC lecture, "Was Freud a Liar?" In that lecture on the seduction theory you provide convincing reasons for concluding that Freud was, in fact, a liar. However, you resist this conclusion. I'm wondering if today you are finally willing to embrace this conclusion.

FC: I'm still not sure that Freud deliberately lied about the seduction episode. I'll tell you what happened. In a review I wrote before that lecture, I actually said that Freud was lying. But then I read an account of Bertrand Russell's explanation of how he came to say that he never advocated preemptive bombing of the Soviet Union, when there was ample evidence to the contrary. Being a great admirer of Russell, I accepted his claim that he had forgotten. In turn, I began to think the same of Freud. That's why I became reluctant to say that Freud lied about the seduction episode. That said, there is ample evidence that he lied on many other matters. So Freud was a liar! He may not have been lying, in 1926, when he reminisced about the seduction episode and said something that was uncontroversially false. But there is one thing that's unequivocal. He said at the time, in 1896, that he did not base his conviction that they had been seduced on anything that they admitted or confessed. Now, he couldn't in later years admit that this was the case, that the seduction theory wasn't based on what they said. Why? Because the seduction stories were, in fact, based on the same kind of material that he was using for the Oedipus complex and his other claims as to infantile sexual life.

If Freud had admitted that his grounds for crediting his reconstruction of infantile life were that the reconstruction made sense of the patient's symptoms, then he would have been faced with the criticism: "Well, that's what you said in 1896, when you got the story completely wrong." So obviously he couldn't admit that, for too much was at stake.

On the other hand, I've heard some people say that Freud was a psychopathic liar. Certainly not. He hated lying. It disturbed him to lie, but it was absolutely necessary if he was to make his way in the world.

AE: I think there were certain details in Freud's later explanations of the seduction theory episode that indicate he must have known that he wasn't telling the truth. I'm not talking just about what he was writing in 1925, but, more specifically, about some of the things he wrote in his first retrospective account of the episode, published in 1906. Those remarks were clearly divergent in some crucial respects from what he wrote in the 1896 papers. I certainly agree with Frank that, by 1925, he probably convinced himself about a certain way of seeing the seduction theory. But in his first retrospective report, he modified—perhaps one should say doctored—his account of what had happened, in order to explain away the clinical claims he had made in 1896 that supposedly corroborated a theory he had since discarded, and, perhaps more importantly—though this was not spelled out—to enable him to justify retaining his analytic reconstructive technique, despite its having resulted in what he later called his "great error." The error is the unequivocal announcement that he had discovered a "source of the Nile" solution to the etiologies of hysteria and obsessional neuroses. In that first retrospective report, we find him maintaining that the problem with the 1896 claims was that the clinical material happened by "chance" to include a disproportionately large number of cases in which there had been sexual abuse by an adult or by older children, but that otherwise his supposed clinical findings were not open to doubt. It was not until his next account, in 1914, that these supposedly numerous authentic cases mysteriously disappeared, to be replaced by patients' unconscious "memories" of early childhood seductions that he came to realize were wish-fulfilling fantasies. How analytic reconstructions of supposed brutal sexual abuse on infants could metamorphose into infants' wishful fantasies of seduction was something he never explained—and, astonishingly, until Frank started asking awkward questions in the 1970s, it was an anomaly that no one seemed to notice.

Incidentally, the widely held view that he abandoned the seduction theory because he came to realize that most of his seduction theory patients had been reporting Oedipal fantasies is manifestly erroneous. In his 1914 report he claimed that he had made the "discovery" that the alleged fantasies were produced to cover up the shameful memories of infantile masturbation. The Oedipal fantasy explanation of the 1896 claims didn't surface until 1925, some thirty years after the episode.

But to return to Frank's point, no doubt Freud deceived himself a great deal of the time about what actually happened. But, equally, there are a number of assertions in his first retrospective report that are so blatantly discrepant with what he wrote in 1896 that he must have known that he was misrepresenting what he had previously claimed.

FC: I would say that the really interesting question is not whether or not Freud lied, but rather, why is it that intellectuals who pride themselves on being tough minded, particularly Freudians trained to confront painful truths, keep repeating the traditional false account of the seduction episode? This was quite excusable twenty-five years ago, because people hadn't had their attention called to the seduction texts. But material long in the public domain now makes it absolutely clear that we cannot accept what Freud said in his later accounts of the seduction error. And there are inconsistencies in what he said in the seduction papers themselves, as well. For example, Freud says that these patients have been abused in the most atrocious ways; for example, they had been anally penetrated. At the same time he says that when these patients remember the episodes, they claim that they thought nothing of it at the time. But how can a child who was being anally penetrated have thought nothing of it? The late Roy Porter, a universally respected medical historian, refused to consider that the traditional seduction accounts are false. Instead, his recent [posthumously published] book continues to repeat conventional material about the seduction error. This is, of course, an ironic situation. People who are supposed to emancipate themselves from idealizations nonetheless hang on to untenable idealizations about Freud and psychoanalysis. The truth is that the psychoanalytic movement as a whole is one of the most corrupt of intellectual movements. It is corrupt due to untenable views being repeated because of personal loyalties and career considerations.

TD: Allen, in *Seductive Mirage*, you certainly undermine the received wisdom about Freud's case studies. But, first of all, how important are these few published cases for psychoanalysis? And, second, does it really matter that they are shot through with inaccuracies?

AE: I can answer this quite briefly! Historically the Freud case histories played a major role in the training of psychoanalysts, but I suspect that this may be rather less the case nowadays. No doubt they are still used to illustrate Freud's interpretative procedures but there is, I think, at least a minimal recognition that the cases were not complete successes, certainly not therapeutically. And of course the Dora case history has been pilloried, even among psychoanalysts, as being undermined by Freud's patriarchal attitudes and his consequent overbearing treatment of his young patient. But this is to let Freud off the hook. What is wrong with the Dora case history is essentially the same as what is wrong with the others: Freud's interpretations and reconstructions throughout the case histories are doubtful, sometimes absurd, inferences based on preconceived theoretical notions. And they are thoroughly unreliable beyond the usual concerns about case histories in general being accounts colored by the distorting lens of the analyst. As fresh information came to light—for example, information supplied by the Wolf-Man—it became evident that supposedly factual material was unreliable. Freud destroyed his original case notes, so it is not possible to ascertain how much distortion occurred in the process of writing up the case histories, but we know from Patrick Mahony's meticulous comparison of the Rat Man case history with the process notes that survived that there were deliberate misrepresentations of the material, in the interests of presenting a coherent analytic narrative—not to mention exaggeration of the efficacy of the treatment.

Of course it matters that the case histories are shot through with inaccuracies. Even if we put aside the dubiousness of so many of the tendentious analytic inferences, how can the case histories not be diminished in value if the supposedly factual material on which some of the inferences rest is itself open to question?

TD: Given both of your critiques of Freud and of Freud studies, what remains, if anything, to be done in the next twenty years as it concerns psychoanalysis?

FC: We still need to explain how it is that the best and brightest in our culture have refused to employ the normal methods of intellectual inquiry when it is a question of Freud. It is a great mistake to think that the present willingness to concede Freud's malfeasances is the result of the scholarship of the last twenty years. Evidence that psychoanalysis wasn't a bona fide inquiry has been available for at least fifty years through a careful scrutiny of Freud's own writings. No very exciting revelations are needed to realize this—no hidden letters, no secret relations with the sister-in-law, and so on. So the fascinating question is why it took so long to come round to a critical view. I would venture that it is partly because Freud has had an enormously beneficial influence, a liberating influence, on twentieth-century culture. For example, we were able to use completely bogus arguments about the baleful effects of sexual repression to get people to ease up, not be so censorious, about other people's sexual lives. That's a great plus. It's a pity that they had to use a phony theory of the neuroses to accomplish this end, but this end is a desirable one nonetheless.

AE: I agree. But it's extraordinarily hard to answer why people have often accepted as factual things for which there is no basis—accepting things, presumably, because they are received historical accounts. In the face of this I think there is still a job to be done correcting time-honored misconceptions about Freud that just won't die. I see myself still trying to refute fallacious material until the more accurate, historically documented picture is more broadly known. For example, the Routledge *Freud Encyclo-*

pedia of 2002 has no less than four entries still peddling the Anna O. phantom pregnancy story, even though this was exposed as bogus more than thirty years ago by material discovered by Ellenberger and by other documents in the public domain. In addition, there are what I call the fairy tale versions of Freud's early analytic career, such as that he induced his patients to recall repressed memories of incidents or ideas that were at the root of somatic symptoms that Freud decided were hysterical, and that this process of—supposedly—bringing forgotten incidents to consciousness resulted, in many cases, in a removal of the symptoms. This is the version one finds in Freud's retrospective accounts of that period, and this story has been recycled in numerous books ever since. Close readings of Freud's publications during the 1890s, however, indicate that for the most part Freud analytically inferred the forgotten memories, and the evidence that he cured the patients of their symptoms is thin. Other practitioners of various therapeutic techniques—before and since—have claimed impressive-sounding cures, but few claims have been taken as literally as Freud's, in part because of his own extraordinarily compelling accounts and the uncritical recycling of them. And, of course, there is no indication of any attempt by Freud to follow up his cases. So in recent years I've been interested in his clinical claims rather more than theoretical issues. I leave that to Frank!

FC: One of the reasons Freud has such a wide constituency is that he has an uncanny knack for being on both sides of almost every question. For example, you get people saying that Freud's greatness consists in his emphasis on the material basis of neurosis. After all, sexuality is something physical. Freud emphasized carnality, and therefore Freud is going to be antipathetic to anyone who wants to sweeten the pill of life—and who wants to side with Jung when ignoring sexuality in the causation of neuroses? On the other hand, there are people who say that Freud despised medical materialism. Thomas Mann says that Freud's greatness, as noted earlier, consists in saying that what we call disease is really something that people do, not something that happens to them. Freud is on both sides of this argument, so how can he lose?

TD: Allen, what do you think about the history of Freud interpretation in the twentieth century?

AE: One thing that struck me from my first serious ventures—in the 1980s—into the literature on Freud was the high regard accorded to the case histories. I thought it extraordinary that so many commentators had read them uncritically, and then reported Freud's supposed findings as if they genuinely revealed the contents of the patients' unconscious mind, and his solutions as if they were valid explanations for the origins of the patients' symptoms. Commentators, with few exceptions prior to the last couple of decades, presumed that they were gaining factual information about what actually happened in the analyses, when what we were actually getting was just Freud's account of his interaction with a patient colored by his interpretative lens. Obviously we have no real idea of what the patient did or thought, and so we have to rely upon what the analyst is telling us. Freud often gave the impression that the material was obtained directly from the patient, when close reading frequently indicates that this was not the case.

I'm not familiar with the writings on Freud prior to World War II, but in the 1940s and 1950s, especially in the United States, his ideas seem to have been widely disseminated in an uncritical manner. This was rather less the case in Britain. I recall only a few isolated writings that inaugurated the postwar challenge to the received view, notably those of Eysenck in the U.K. and Salter in the U.S. In Britain, where the psychiatric profession was less infatuated with Freud, the debate—inspired by Eysenck's provocative contentions—tended to be around the efficacy of psychoanalysis as a therapy. Of course there had always been offshoots of mainstream Freudian psychoanalysis that rejected one or another element of the orthodox view, but I don't think it was until the latter part of the twentieth century that mainstream psychoanalysts deviated in appreciable numbers from major parts of the Freud edifice.

Within the psychoanalytic movement itself, some basic notions in Freud's writings came to be rejected, most notably those on female sexuality. But much of this was a recognition of the changing social context, rather than a critical evaluation of the writings in question. What was lacking within the psychoanalytic fold was a realization that the explanation for the deficiencies in Freud's claims about female psychosexual development was precisely the same as for those in relation to males—namely, that Freud developed his theories first and only then purported to validate them by tendentious analytic interpretations in the clinical setting. How else does one explain that, although in the earlier period of his career Freud's patients were predominantly female, as late as 1925 he was still basing his notions of psychosexual development on—supposed—early-childhood male experiences? Psychoanalysts have argued that Freud's views on female development were colored by the prejudices of his time, but this will not do. Freud claimed to have a clinical procedure that almost infallibly revealed the contents of his patients' unconscious. Why should this be any less efficacious with women than with men? The truth is that his theories of psychosexual development for both males and females lacked a sound empirical basis from the start—but this is something psychoanalysts are loathe to acknowledge, because it would undermine much of the rationale for the traditional foundations of psychoanalysis.

TD: So, Frank, what good has psychoanalysis done for interpretation in the twentieth century?

FC: For people who practice interpretation it has done them a lot of good, since it gave them a template on which they could model their utterances. As far as helping us understand the phenomena being interpreted—if you are so reactionary as to believe that there is something to understand and that we can't just say whatever we like—I think psychoanalysis has probably done more harm than good. We've had more stupidity, more silliness, than we've had insight.

TD: Any advice for the interpreters of Freud?

FC: If by interpreters of Freud you mean those who are trying to make use of Freudian theory for hermeneutic ends, then my advice is that they should be more reflexive as to what they are doing and should ask basic questions. What is somebody doing when he or she interprets? Why do people interpret? What is the satisfaction they get out of it? One kind of interpreting is just a process of assimilating the cultural artifacts that surround us to our own world of intellectual loyalties. If we are Marxists, then we will put a Marxist gloss on them. If we are feminists, a feminist gloss. Freudians, a Freudian gloss, and so on. But I don't think we are doing anything essentially different than what a medieval Catholic was doing when he said that the three-leafed clover was a manifestation of the Trinity. The interesting question is, why was he doing that? If you ask that question, then you are on your way to understanding why Freudians, feminists, and Marxists are doing what they are doing. I would ask these intellectuals to consider the following comparison: ethologists say that when dogs seem to be urinating, they are not really urinating but are marking out an area as belonging to them. They are placing their mark on something. That, bluntly put, is what I think intellectuals in the twentieth century have been doing when they interpret material: they have been lifting their legs and marking the material as belonging to Freud, or to Marx, or to Melanie Klein, or to whomever.

TD: [*laughing*] A final softball for Allen: can we now say that Freud is dead?

AE: I think we can separate the question into two parts. I doubt that many psychiatrists nowadays take seriously the theories of the origins of psychological and emotional disorders found in Freud's writings. More generally, I think that many of the foundational notions in Freud's edifice have been either rejected or simply put aside within the psychological profession. On the other hand, aside from self-acknowledged psychoanalysts, many psychotherapists remain attached to Freud's interpretative devices, and this is unlikely to change much in the foreseeable future. But in comparison with the position he once held as probably the most revered name in psychology, I think that there has been an irreversible change of view about his achievements and that this process of reevaluation will continue.

Interestingly enough, the use of Freudian notions in some parts of the academy, notably in humanistic disciplines, has probably never been more extensive than in recent decades. My view is that this is the case because this kind of interpretative theorizing lends itself to all manner of plausible, and not-so-plausible, explanations of human behavior, and this is not a feature that some humanistic scholars will relinquish lightly. Likewise, in general cultural terms, the propensity to look for plausible explanations of behavior is likely to ensure that *Freud* remains a byword for our understanding of human behavior among the general public for some time to come, though it is likely to be increasingly challenged in the public consciousness by notions originating from evolutionary psychology. But just how long this battle of explanations will take to work itself through to a rough consensus—if it ever does—is anybody's guess.

Addendum, 2005:
Cioffi on Cioffi, Freud, and Pseudoscience

TD: Let me ask you again: do you still think that although Freud may have lied on some occasions, he may not have been lying in his later accounts of the seduction episode?

FC: I now find my conclusion in the first interview confused—the claim that Freud was not lying—since what I go on to say extenuates the lie I deny he told! Allen makes a good case that Freud lied about the seduction episode and did not merely misremember. What I would still maintain, though, is that the cover-up is of much greater interest than the offense. The list of those who misrepresented what an hour in a library would have set them straight on includes the most celebrated of Freud commentators.

A piquant example of the strength of the prevailing sycophancy is provided by Adolf Grünbaum, who intersperses his objections to psychoanalysis with fulsome testimony to Freud's integrity as an uncommonly candid investigator who was "hospitable to adverse evidence." What grounds does Grünbaum [1984] offer for this hospitality? Freud's abandonment of the seduction theory. He does not ask how Freud was able to establish that a patient had in fact not suffered infantile sexual abuse. Nor does he ask how Freud justified his retention of his reconstructive method which led to the seduction theory when it had proved so blatantly erroneous. What matters is not what Freud abandoned, but what he retained—his pretensions to preternatural reconstructive powers remained intact and so he was not hospitable to adverse evidence as Grünbaum maintained.

TD: What made you think that Popper's untestability wasn't the answer to the problem of demarcating genuine science from pseudoscience?

FC: The song says that they liked New York so much that they named it twice. Karl Popper liked his criterion of demarcation so much that he named it three times: falsifiability, testability, refutability. So he obviously had great hopes for it. Popper wobbled between two senses of untestable—a formal, logical sense and a pragmatic, methodological one. And I thought that the second captures better what it is we are trying to convey when we describe Freud and his acolytes as pseudoscientists. I called my view capitulationism [Cioffi 1998a]. It is not the untestability of Freud's theses, but rather, our feeling that he has wantonly refused to capitulate to "falsificatory" evidence that incites us to label him a pseudoscientist.

But there is a role for formal untestability as well. The question of whether a theory is testable is a matter of great moment when it has repeatedly been declared to have been tested and survived, and this is disputed. When we then discover that—with respect to their most distinctive theses, for example, the infantile sexual etiology—neither Freud nor his followers have any clear notion of what such possible falsificatory evidence would consist in, we reach for pejorative epistemic terms, of which *pseudoscience* is the most familiar, though really infelicitous. It would be better to call Freud's clinical enterprise pseudobiographical or pseudohermeneutic. My change of view led to a division between me and those who saw no reason to modify Popper's view.

The main reason for their unwillingness to take up my attitude towards untestability is that it was felt too indulgent. I did not object to untestability in itself but only where it was coupled with spurious claims that the theory had been tested and survived. Where the theory was candidly untestable I was not disposed to deploy pejorative epistemic terms. I preferred to call such untestable theories protoscientific rather than pseudoscientific. I was no longer concerned to regulate what people believed but only what they claimed to know.

TD: Could you say something more about the distinction between protoscience and pseudoscience as it applies to Freud?

FC: Sure. Consider the case of Freud's account of infantile sexual life and imagine we were confronted with someone who said that he was convinced that what Freud said about it was correct—for example, about voluptuous defecation and its influence on character formation—but that he had to concede that with the means of investigation at our disposal at present we could not determine whether or not the situation was as Freud described it. I would insist on distinguishing this case from that with which we are more often confronted—of Freudians' maintaining that his theory was not a mere speculation but had survived all attempts to disprove it.

One of the advantages of my capitulationist construal of untestability is that it makes one source of the dispute over the status of psychoanalysis more intelligible. For it is well known that genuine investigators are often reluctant to capitulate to apparent falsifiers and adopt all sorts of devices for clinging to their theory, and sometimes they are proved right in the end. There doesn't seem to be a coercive rule for resolving disputes which arise on this score, and so it is not surprising when the issue remains unresolved since what is really at issue is the good faith of the investigator—and this does not lend itself to demonstration.

And I soon realized that capitulationism had other deficiencies. Not only is the failure to capitulate not sufficient to brand someone a pseudoscientist, but his capitulation is not sufficient to absolve him of the charge.

Grünbaum assumed that it was. He argued—with characteristic exegetical irresponsibility—that Freud often capitulated to empirical evidence and so must be exonerated from Popper's accusation of dogmatism. Not everyone has been impressed by this argument. Freud may have been like Big Jule in *Guys and Dolls*, someone who thinks it's permissible to shoot craps with blank dice because he has memorized the position of the dots. Ought we to see Freud as responsive to adverse evidence because, like Big Jule, he sometimes announces that he has failed to make his point? In fact, even if Freud's capitulationism was more than a fantasy of Grünbaum's it would not exonerate him. There is another criterion which an investigator must meet if he is to be exonerated: he must answer the charge that he is guilty of spurious instantiation reports—and I mean spurious, not merely mistaken. That is, if someone announces that all swans are rainbow-colored and that he has seen dozens of them, and then when a white swan is produced admits that he has overgeneralized his results, he has still to satisfy us that he had at least prima facie adequate grounds for his rainbow-colored swan reports. Capitulation is not enough.

This is why I feel the issues raised by Allen Esterson [1996] over Freud's particular claims in his case histories are more pertinent than the ones raised by philosophers of science as to the testability of Freud's law-like utterances.

TD: There is also an issue between you and other critics of Freud, like Morris Eagle [1998], over the relevance of the behavior of the theorist to the stigmatization of his theory as pseudoscientific.

FC: The most common mistake made by Freud critics is their preoccupation with the strictly logical implications of his theses. They may be extrapolating from relatively infrequent cases where there are such strict implications. But with the most distinctive Freudian theses—for instance, those pertaining to infancy and to sexuality—you cannot proceed directly to derivations. You must work out from the response of advocates of the theses to objections what if anything they consider falsificatory. We can't keep the theorist out of the theory. Grünbaum, for example, thinks Freud committed to the thesis that there can be no homosexual paranoid. Perhaps he is right, but he does not derive this from psychoanalytic theory. He attributes this view to Freud because Freud expressed it. In other words, he was using the very biographical criterion he inveighs against in his blather about "the theory in itself" [see Grünbaum, 1984: 110].

TD: That may show some advocates of testability to be inconsistent. But what of the substantive issue?

FC: Apart from this inconsistency there are other objections to formalism. Morris Eagle [1998] criticized Crews for not distinguishing "the methodological practices and attitudes of individual analysts (including Freud) and the independent logical structure of psychoanalytic theory." Eagle maintained that what mattered is "whether or not certain psychoanalytic propositions can be treated as authentic hypotheses."

This view is parasitic for its plausibility on the unstated assumption that the psychoanalytic propositions in question have enough evidence in their favor to be worth treating as "authentic hypotheses." Otherwise, Eagle would have to explain why he is not calling for the research into the theses of Scientology or Christian Science. If the probity or judiciousness of those who have reported sightings of a sea monster in Loch Ness is of no moment, but only the in-principle detectability of such a creature, then why aren't we looking for it in Windermere or Lake Huron?

TD: You have also been charged with taking an overindulgent attitude toward the argument that analysts could not reasonably be expected to produce for public consumption all the evidence they have in favor of their reconstructions and interpretations.

FC: There are areas of discourse in which judgments are made and deferred to in spite of the fact that the publicly transmissible grounds for them are acknowledged to be inadequate—for example, medicine and connoisseurship. What gives these judgments their authority is not their grounds, but their source. "Berenson says it is not a Raphael"; "The great diagnostician says that the patient, although manifesting none of the normal signs of a disease, nevertheless has the disease." In these cases we accept their judgments in the absence of ponderable evidence because, in general, their judgments have been so often vindicated by ponderable evidence; in fact, insight has been defined as "successful invalid inference." Now this is the claim made for Freud's reconstructions and general views on infantile sexuality, and they can't be impugned except by impugning the trustworthiness or discernment of those who made them.

This is why I concluded my piece for the Freud Library of Congress exhibit with the statement that "psychoanalysis is a testimonial science" [Cioffi 1998b]. The paramount importance of getting the seduction episode right is that it shows that Freud's testimony or judgment or both cannot be relied on—and incidentally, that his acolytes cannot be depended on to give an accurate account of his grounds for first crediting and then deserting the seduction theory.

TD: Since, unlike other critics of psychoanalytic explanation, you deny that what is wrong is their failure to meet the same criteria as any scientific explanation, why do you stigmatize them as spurious?

FC: I call them spurious because they fail to meet the appropriate humanistic criteria so blatantly that they deserve to be called fraudulent rather than just mistaken.

TD: How do you show that?

FC: Let's look at a credible example of humanistic explanation, say, the case of eccentricities of the spinster Miss Havisham in *Great Expectations*. Among these were her being garbed in a wedding dress, wearing only one white shoe, and having all the clocks in her house stopped at twenty to nine. The explanation turns out to be that, on what was to have been her wedding day, she received, at twenty to nine while dressed in the manner described, the news that she had been duped by her fiancé and he had absconded.

The philosophical significance of this specimen is that it would be sheer scientism to object that it is unsupported by a law. It is an example of jigsaw reasoning. The right objection to Freudian explanation is not as Grünbaum and others would have it—that they cannot appeal to established laws—but that they don't meet the Miss Havisham standard of circumstantialities or anything like it.

So we should not allow ourselves to be sidelined into the issue of whether Freudian explanation ought to be expected to meet scientific standards. We should ask instead: are any of the hundreds of clinical reports illustrative of Freudian theory circumstantially warranted? Put succinctly: are there Freudian phenomena? Because, if there are, then he made discoveries so remarkable that it betrays a churlish ingratitude to protest that they are not lawlike in the manner demanded in science. If there is one authenticated instance of a displacement upwards induced by an unconscious mechanism, so that a girl's fantasies about being deflowered can result in a migraine headache—and dozens have been reported—then Freud is indeed the great discoverer he was claimed to be. The same goes for the influence of infantile sexual life. If there is one authentic case of an infant's transaction with his feces determining his adult attitude to money, then Freud deserves great credit for having discovered this.

TD: In the peer-group review of Grünbaum's *The Foundations of Psychoanalysis* [1984], you chose to restrict your remarks to a criticism of his claim that Freud appealed to therapeutic effect to meet objections. Grünbaum's reply charged you with manufacturing nonexistent texts to support your case. How do you respond to this?

FC: I won't say anything about the tally argument itself because Allen Esterson (1996) has comprehensively dealt with the issue in an article.[1] I will just mention some of the considerations which I adduced in my peer-group comment, and my reason for thinking Grünbaum's response to them disreputable as well as mistaken. One of my arguments was that Freud could not plausibly invoke therapeutic effect as validation of his clinical method and data since he had publicly claimed countless therapeutic successes before having arrived at the etiologies for which, on Grünbaum's view, he thought himself entitled to claim therapeutic validation.

Another argument I advanced is this: if Freud had external validation of speculations initially based on clinical impressions, as he repeatedly claimed, then why would he need to resort to dubious claims of therapeutic superiority for epistemic underwriting of his theory of infantile sexuality or for the validity of his method? This is what Freud says: "It is gratifying to be able to report that direct observation has fully confirmed the results arrived at through psychoanalysis—which is incidentally good evidence of the trustworthiness of that method of research" [Freud 1905, 193n2]. Grünbaum falls back on an "I never said that" defense. The therapeutic validation he imputed to Freud did not extend to matters like infantile sexuality. Grünbaum seems to have as much difficulty in construing his own prose as the rest of us. And what use would the tally argument be to Freud if he could not use it in his polemics over his most contested claims?

Lest my claim that Grünbaum's dealings with my objections were disreputable appear intemperate and self-serving, let me quote what a disinterested third party, F. Kraupl-Taylor, the editor of *Psychological Medicine*, said editorially about Grünbaum's dealings with my criticism: "Even

---

1. It has been a decade since Grünbaum announced that he would demolish its arguments—but Esterson is still waiting.

Grünbaum when in hot pursuit of a debating point could stray from the narrow path of sound reasoning and plunge into an obvious blunder. This happened in his long reply to Cioffi, whom he accused of failing to adduce textual documentation." The blunder Kraupl-Taylor is referring to is Grünbaum's refutation of my claim that, far from relying on Grünbaum's tally argument for empirical support, Freud found his most irrefragable proof in the productions of dements and paranoiacs. Grünbaum looked up the word *irrefragable* in a concordance to Freud's works and could find nothing to support my view. Kraupl-Taylor pointed out that since Freud wrote in German and not English, Grünbaum could hardly expect to find the relevant passage in this way [Kraupl-Taylor 1987]. This is the Freud passage I was referring to, and it is from the same lecture on which Grünbaum based his own thesis: "Nor must we fail to point out that a large number of the individual findings of analysis, which might otherwise be suspected of being products of suggestion, are confirmed from another irreproachable source. Our guarantors in this case are the sufferers from dementia praecox and paranoia" [Freud 1916–1917, 453].

And wasn't Kraupl-Taylor being excessively charitable when he called Grünbaum's failure to find the passage by looking up my term *irrefragable* a "blunder"? Wasn't it just a ruse to give the impression that a quotation which undermined his thesis had been invented by me?

TD: Looking at our original interview, is there anything else you would like to withdraw besides your amnesia theory of Freud's misrepresentation of the seduction episode?

FC: Well, I became aware that several judgments will strike a neutral reader as overstated. I am thinking of my denunciation of the psychoanalytic movement as "one of the most corrupt." Without supporting evidence, the judgment must strike a reader as gratuitous and scurrilous. What I meant to convey is my suspicion that the criteria of acceptance employed by analysts was so often the social-professional status of those who made the assertions, rather than any empirical support they might have had, and that later modifications of Freud's theory were the outcome of market research, rather than empirical inquiry. Isn't there ground for the suspicion that theses were only abandoned when some powerful constituency—homosexual or feminist—protested?

There is another reason for general suspicion of the contemporary analytic community. Although fewer and fewer Freudian apologists are now willing to stand by the authenticity of many of Freud's distinctive discoveries, none has been willing to address the question as to how it came about that phenomena they now concede not to occur were reported so consistently over so long a period.

But I guess my strongest reason for imputing corruption is related to my thesis as to the untestability of much of psychoanalytic theory. The bearing of this on the corruption issue is that when revisionists assure us that they have abandoned those theses—on which the critics based their dismissal of Freudian theory—they have inadvertently exposed their opportunism. For given the epistemic character of the abandoned theses, they can have had no empirical grounds for abandoning them.

TD: How do you account for the fact that there are critics of Freud who do not reject him as unreservedly as you?

FC: I think they are implicitly appealing to trade-off considerations. Wittgenstein spoke of the great disservice performed by Freud's "fanciful pseudo-explanations": "Now any ass has these pictures available to use in 'explaining' symptoms" [Wittgenstein 1980, 56]. And it is true that there are Freudians who concede the occasional asininity of Freudian interpretations but think it outweighed by his achievements. But if the force of Wittgenstein's "Now any ass" thesis is to be countered, then some way must be found of calculating asininity-insight ratios so that it can be determined that we have gained more than we have lost by deploying Freud's hermeneutic patrimony. Thomas Nagel [1994] speaks of the "evident usefulness of a rudimentary Freudian outlook." Whatever usefulness it may have must be weighed against the plethora of instances like that of a celebrated training analyst's explanation of a patient's "feeling a depression"—namely, in terms of a childhood castration trauma occasioned when sexual curiosity led him to put his hand between a little girl's thighs and he felt, not as he had vaguely anticipated, a phallus like his own, but "a depression." A familiar psychodynamic mechanism then transformed the memory of the tactually perceived depression into the adult experience of depression [see Sharpe 1937, 32].

Is it enough to say of such discourse, as Thomas Nagel does, that it is a fruitful extension of commonsense psychology and that we must reconcile ourselves to its fallibility? An intellectual community which encourages such a mode of discourse deserves to be judged harshly.

TD: What about your remarks on the sources of Freud's appeal?

FC: I don't have much to withdraw as to what I said about the sources of Freud's attractiveness, but there is much I would like to add. I have argued that Freud enjoyed a specially protected status in our culture. The evidence for this kind of thesis is bound to be impressionistic and anecdotal. In my book, *Freud and the Question of Pseudoscience* [1998a], I compared the status of Freudian psychoanalysis with that of the operation of Jim Crow in the northern states in which I grew up, in that those who had not witnessed its operation firsthand, and whose lifetime was post–civil rights, found the degree of segregation difficult to imagine and would not find the existing documentation commensurate with the experienced reality. There is another point of similarity between the two movements of racism and psychoanalysis in that the episodes were so shameful that there is a tendency to self-protectively understate the extent of general participation.

So here are some anecdotal illustrations of Freud's specially protected status in the intellectual community. Ernst Gombrich, who I invited to contribute to my Macmillan volume on Freud [in 1973 for their Modern Judgements series], wrote to say that he would first want to know who the other contributors were as he had good friends among Freudians and did not wish to appear in unseemly company. I did not send him the list of contributors but preferred to dispense with his contribution. When I was invited by the analyst Tom Main to participate in a BBC series on Freud in which the Kleinian Hannah Segal was to represent psychoanalysis, the condition was imposed that I would not put questions to her directly, but that they would be relayed through Main. One of my questions was on the testability of Freud's infantile etiology. She dealt with it brusquely by pointing out that if a young child was taken from his mother and showed no sign of distress she would concede that Freud's theory had been falsified. Why not throw the child in the air and concede that if it stayed there Freud's theory was falsified? You can see why she did not wish to be questioned directly, but why was this condition acceded to? More recently, there was the episode of the *Partisan Review*'s publishing an article [by Nathan Hale] complaining of the irrational bias of Freud's critics, but then refusing them a right of reply on the ground that the issues were too esoteric for their readers. Since the main issue was whether one of the iconic figures of our culture, renowned for his honesty, was in fact untruthful and disingenuous, how could this fail to be of general interest? I think we are entitled to conclude that the grounds given were bogus and that the editors were determined that the case against Freud not be heard. Since there is a pronounced tendency to understate the intimidatory standing Freud enjoys, I am glad to put some corrective considerations on record.

TD: To what does Freud owe his protected status?

FC: In part to the notion that our discreditable impulses are unconscious. Far from being troubling, the unconscious is welcomed because it spares us the pain of confronting how much in consciousness is perverse and contemptibly egoistic. I invite the reader to perform the following experiment to persuade him of the attractiveness of the Freudian thesis that our perverse and ferociously egoistic impulses are unconscious. Which of these thoughts is more troubling: "I find myself so attracted to my daughter that I have sometimes find myself incipiently erectile in her presence" or "My analyst has convinced me that I have an unconscious incestuous attraction to my daughter"?

I acknowledge, of course, that much of the veneration extended Freud is purely conventional. What is sometimes at work is the familiar mechanism which makes people go to McDonald's to eat its hamburgers. Once an everybody's-doing-it status is annexed to an idea, the appeal of its own distinctive features may become nugatory or inert. As the cynical adage has it, "A dog's obeyed in office." And though this explains why so many express veneration for Freud, nevertheless the intrinsic appeal of his views must also play a role—otherwise how did the dog get into office in the first place?

So the question cannot be evaded. What is this intrinsic appeal? Resolving this question will make less baffling the sentiment expressed by Elaine Showalter in a review [June 12, 1997] of Crews for *The Guardian*, in which she objected that Crews is "helpless to explain why so many intelligent people will concede all of his criticisms and yet refuse to abandon their general loyalty to Freud." I have some suggestions as to the source of this general loyalty. Freud has become a symbol for so much that is liberating that it is almost impossible to criticize him without provoking passionate resentment on the part of people who would find it difficult to give any coherent account of what it is that he maintained.

TD: Recall that, in the earlier interview, you said that "Freud has had an enormously beneficial influence, a liberating influence, on twentieth-century culture"—and this despite aspects of his theory being "completely bogus." Is there a contradiction here?

FC: I think I can reduce the appearance of contradiction by being more specific about the direction from which the benefit came. It was through its direct effect on sexual mores and attitudes, and not through its enabling us to better understand or treat mental illness, that Freud's ideas exerted a beneficent influence. If psychoanalytic discourse were accurately described as a theory of the unconscious, most of us would have never heard of it. It is in large measure due to its trafficking in images of penises and anuses and semen and nipples and vulvas—but in a distancing, scientific mode—that its prominence in our discursive transactions with mental life and cultural life in general is to be explained. The influence of Freud has been compared to that of Kinsey by Simon and Gagnon [1974]: "When the Kinsey studies reported that very large numbers of people masturbated, other men who had done so felt better." The same thing goes for the range of perversities that Freud has naturalized.

Jerome Bruner [1973] wrote that Freud "has tempered the spirit of punitiveness towards what we took as evil and what we now see as sick" [144]. Nothing would be more salutary than for the sexually intolerant among us to be converted to a "there but for the grace of God" attitude toward homosexuals—or toward any noncriminal deviance. Although we might have drawn on our Christian tradition for this tolerance ("Let he who is without sin," et cetera), it seems that we got it from Freud—though of course his views were not ideally enlightened. He saw homosexuals as freaks, although not morally reprehensible ones.

TD: In *The Black Book of Psychoanalysis*, published in France in September of 2005, you contribute some words of skepticism about the likelihood that we will be able to free ourselves from Freud.

FC: Yes—and Crews, Esterson, and Borch-Jacobsen all disagree with me! I argued that, for all of our efforts to demonstrate how idealized the current image of Freud is and how much baseness there was in the movement he founded, it would make no long-term difference to his standing, that his theory would continue to provide comfort and the illusion of understanding to almost as many as it traditionally has. He will never become just a coterie figure like Gurdjiev, Ouspenski, L. Ron Hubbard, or Count Alfred Korzybski.

I think that Freud's status in our culture is not a negotiable issue and that it is as foolish to think that we could bring about an end to his ritual veneration as that we can prevent our public figures from regularly invoking the deity. Only posterity will know who is right about this, of course, but let me provide some grounds for maintaining that Freud will continue to be venerated—in *secula seculorum*. What we get from some current apologists is an assurance of what a splendid chap Freud was when he wasn't selling used cars, which he might well have been. This will result in a permanent division between the attitude of those who bought a used car from Freud and those who didn't. And the former will eventually die out. It's true that not all justifications for honoring Freud are nonepistemic in this rag-trade "never-mind-the-truth, feel-the-quality" mode, and that many will continue to insist on his epistemic achievement and not just his literary powers. But the terms in which this epistemic justification for his greatness are expressed are so rarefied as to be out of reach of rational assessment. Freud, it is now suggested, is not the successor to Copernicus and Darwin—as he himself held—but to Sophocles and Plato! Look at Jonathan Lear's [1995] apologetic—and that of Elaine Showalter, Thomas Nagel, and Stuart Hampshire—and ask yourself whether it will ever be unavailable to anyone who wishes to resort to it. Why should things change?

7

Schreber, Seduction, and Scholarship:
Han Israëls on Idiots, Lunatics, and the
Psychopathology of Freud Scholars

Interviewed by Mikkel Borch-Jacobsen and Sonu Shamdasani

Han Israëls received his PhD in sociology from the University of Amsterdam and now teaches psychology and law at the University of Maastricht in Holland. Israëls is best known for his work on Daniel Paul Schreber, who was the presiding Senatspräsident of the high court of Saxony when, in 1893, he began a long descent into mental illness. Freud wrote a highly speculative case study about Schreber in 1911, and, ever since, scholars have gone both with and against the grain of psychoanalysis to better understand Schreber's illness. In addition to his *Schreber: Father and Son* of 1989, Israëls has published on other aspects of Freud's work, including the seduction theory, his research on cocaine, his booklet on Leonardo, and the case of Hermine Hug-Hellmuth. Israëls's latest book, *The Freud Case*, is not yet available in English.

Mikkel Borch-Jacobsen and Sonu Shamdasani conducted the interview in London on August 19, 1993, and the editor and Israëls updated it in August 2005. Borch-Jacobsen was interviewed for this book in Chapter 8. Shamdasani is a prominent Jung scholar whose books include *Jung and the Making of Modern Psychology* (2003) and *Cult Fictions: C. G. Jung and the Founding of Analytic Psychology* (1998).

. . .

MB-J/SS: How did you first become interested in Freud's work? How does one become a Freud scholar?

HI: I was studying sociology in Amsterdam and was looking for an idea for my final dissertation. My thesis director advised me to take a look at a book written by Morton Schatzman on the Schreber case, entitled *Soul Murder* [1973]. At that time, I didn't even know who Schreber was—I mean Paul Schreber, the son of Moritz Schreber and the subject of Freud's study. At any rate, this choice had to do with historic, sociological ideas about how the personality structure in Western culture has changed over the centuries and how certain theories about education might be interesting in that respect. My Amsterdam professor thought that Schreber's father's theories about education, as described by Schatzman, might be a good topic for me. I tried to work along those lines, but at the same time I quickly did something which now, looking back, I think was completely foolish. I decided that if I wanted to write something about Moritz Schreber and his son Paul, I had to go and see the places where these people had lived, in the former Kingdom of Saxony. So I took the train and went to Leipzig, in what was at that time still the German Democratic Republic. There I had a lot of luck, for I managed to find, almost by accident, some of the descendants of the Schreber family. They were very proud of their ancestors but didn't know anything at all about one of them being one of the most famous cases in the history of psychiatry. They had still kept a lot of material about their ancestors and when I got access to it, I realized that for the first time in my life I knew certain things that nobody else knew. I quickly decided to abandon my sociological approach and to start writing my PhD on this new historical material. That's how I came into the field.

MB-J/SS: Before you, every commentator on the case had initially approached Schreber through the lens of Freud. Would you say that the way in which you came to Schreber first rather than coming to Schreber through Freud shaped the distinctiveness of your work?

HI: Well, yes, I did not come to Schreber through Freud. I came to Schreber independently of psychoanalysis. Of course, everybody realizes that Freud is decisive for all this literature, but I found, and in fact I still think, that Freud's essay on the Schreber case is not so very interesting, not so very brilliant, not so very well written. Freud has done other things that are much better. Anyway, I have not worked much on what Freud wrote about the Schreber case. My work has focused primarily on what later authors wrote about the Schreber case, especially William Niederland, who, around 1960, published several important articles that have been republished in a book called *The Schreber Case* [1984], and Morton Schatzman—and on the whole controversy that was stirred up by their publications.

MB-J/SS: In his work, Freud proceeds via single cases, such as Schreber. Would you say that, methodologically, he's completely wrong right at the outset?

HI: I don't know. We can safely assume that when Freud wrote down his analysis of the Schreber case, he already had the idea that paranoia is the result of repressed homosexuality. He had that idea before he read Schreber's *Memoirs* [1903]. We know this because he says it in a letter to Jung [October 1, 1910], and we also know that he got that idea from his own reaction to what had happened with Wilhelm Fliess. So you could say that Freud did not even base his theory of paranoia on the analysis of Schreber's *Memoirs*. He analyzed his own case and then projected it onto Schreber's case. Now, looking at your own self in order to get an idea and then trying to find arguments to back it, that's of course an excellent procedure from a heuristic point of view. The idea, the initial hypothesis, can come from everywhere. But single cases cannot prove anything.

MB-J/SS: Freud, of course, thought they could.

HI: Yes, but you can't call that a proof. Freud's interpretation of the Schreber case is plausible, but other interpretations, like Schatzman's, for example, are at least as plausible, although they don't prove anything either.

MB-J/SS: What do you mean?

HI: Schatzman's hypothesis is that Schreber's paranoia is not the result of repressed homosexuality but of real persecution in his childhood. The advantage of this interpretation is that it is simpler than Freud's and that it is, in many aspects, very specific. Schatzman, elaborating on discoveries that were made by Niederland, was able to show all sorts of parallels between the curious contraptions used by Schreber's father and the "supernatural" things happening to Schreber's son in his delirium. This gives a certain plausibility to the idea that there is a link between persecution during childhood and mental patients' feelings of persecution. But again, it doesn't prove much. In order to prove this hypothesis, you would need to study more cases. Although I like Schatzman's book, I think that there is a simpler explanation for the return of these childhood events in Schreber's delirium. If you are mentally ill and you have all kinds of fantasies and delusions, these must come from somewhere. Obviously, they don't come from reality, since they aren't real in the normal sense of the word. So they must come from your brain, from your memory, that is to say, from what you have experienced in your life. Things that happened in your life are bound to come back in the delirium; it can't be otherwise. But that doesn't necessarily mean that they are the cause of the mental illness. Maybe the mental illness has a completely different cause. Maybe something purely organic has gone wrong.

According to Schatzman, Moritz Schreber's mechanical devices had been used very widely in Germany in those days, so one would expect that many more people would have gone mad as a result. Schatzman would probably reply that these contraptions had been used much more in Schreber's case than in the case of other German children. Sure, but the fact of the matter is that a real proof in this area is nearly impossible. What Schatzman did is interesting, just as what Freud did is interesting, but it doesn't even come close to an effort to try to prove something. My own research doesn't either.

MB-J/SS: Then what's the point?

HI: There is no point. I'm doing historical research and as a result of that research we know a little bit more about these people than we did before.

MB-J/SS: And that's it?

HI: Well, yes—that's it. If you want to know more about the causes of mental illness, I think you shouldn't do historical research.

MB-J/SS: However, you argue that it is more plausible to suggest there is an organic basis.

HI: What I say there is that I'm an outsider. I'm not a psychiatrist and I read the psychiatric literature on the Schreber case with the eyes of a layman. Now, I was not impressed by the level of that literature. It was not very scientific. There were people trying to argue in favor of specific points of view, but it seemed to me that they were more interested in trying to prove their own point than in finding the truth. Judging from all that psychiatric literature, I got the impression that genetic research, at least, was more seriously done. But remember, I wrote this in 1980. Today I would simply shut up, for I really don't know. I'm not a specialist and we've learned that even scientific fraud also sometimes exists in this field. So I wouldn't dare to make general statements. I consider my work as historical work, not as a research on the causes of schizophrenia or of mental illness.

MB-J/SS: So would you consider yourself as a professional debunker, as a sheer negativist?

HI: Listen, I'm just doing historical work. I'm trying to find out what happened to interesting people like Freud, his followers, and his patients, just as somebody else might do research on Jesus Christ, or Stalin, or Napoleon.

MB-J/SS: Historians always have agendas.

HI: I didn't have a hidden agenda at the beginning, if that is what you mean. But it's true that I gradually got one. I was especially interested in seeing how the psychoanalysts had reacted to Schatzman's book on the Schreber case. Their reaction struck me because they were unfair in dealing with Schatzman to a measure that was unknown to me up till then. That caused me to get interested not only in what had happened in the lives of the Schreber father and son, but also in the scientific discussion about them. So I became more and more interested in psychoanalysis as a scientific field or, rather, as a field that pretends to be scientific.

MB-J/SS: Did you still approach this new research as a sociologist on the track of the civilizing process?

HI: No. In what I'm doing now, there is no sociology anymore. There is just a curiosity about how unfairly people deal with each other in this so-called scientific field. This doesn't have anything to do with sociology. It has to do with plain common sense, with the decency that we normally expect from scientists. To take an example, when Niederland wrote his book on the Schreber case, it is quite obvious that he wrote it in reaction to Schatzman's book. It's easy to prove. But Schatzman's book is not even mentioned in the bibliography! Now, this is very interesting from the point of view that we, late twentieth-century intellectuals, still have of psychoanalysis. We think of it as being a respectable field of research, in which decent people have civilized, scholarly discussions. But as I found out when working on the discussion around Schreber, the reality is quite different.

MB-J/SS: What is your view on Niederland's [1984] book, and in particular on the way in which he unearthed potentially devastating material on Freud's case, yet seemed to protect Freud at the same time?

HI: Niederland is the one who found out about the parallels between these contraptions of Schreber's father and his son's hallucinations, and this was without a doubt a major discovery. At the same time, it is unclear to what extent this discovery can be combined with a firm belief in what Freud wrote about the Schreber case. Niederland was describing Schreber's father as a sadist, as somebody who had, to say the least, a very harsh, unfriendly way of educating children. As for Freud, he did not pay very much attention to Schreber's father, but what he did write about him was fairly positive: he described him as a successful educationist and as an "excellent father" [Freud 1911, 78]. Now, Niederland, who had written extensively about Freud's interpretation of the Schreber case, kept completely silent about this discrepancy with his own interpretation. This attempt to hide the fact that he had views that were very different from Freud is just another example of what is fundamentally wrong with postwar psychoanalysis. At any rate, this attitude of Niederland's, combined with the way he treated Schatzman, was so unscientific that I found it interesting in itself. Of course, at first I thought this was something specific to Niederland or to a limited group of psychoanalysts.

MB-J/SS: What, in your view, does it tell us about psychoanalysis?

HI: Well, it tells something about Niederland and, in as far as the discussion with Schatzman is concerned, it also tells something about, say, twenty or thirty of his colleagues. So it really begins to tell something about American psychoanalysis in the 1970s.

MB-J/SS: We know that intellectual priority is a hot issue in scientific research in general. What is so special about Freud studies in this regard?

HI: The academic world is full of idiots, to be sure, but it seems that few fields attract so many idiots and lunatics as the field of Freud research. If you go to a lecture on Freud, you can be sure that, when it comes to the questions, several people in the audience will turn out to be complete idiots. For some reason, Freud appeals to people who are somewhere on the boundary between lunacy, madness, and genius. It has certainly to do with the subjects about which Freud writes, but there are other reasons too. One of them, I think, is that this is mainly a nonacademic field of research. There are a few people in the field who hold a university position, like Peter Gay, but most Freud scholars do not have jobs at a university. Now, this explains many things in Freud studies. When you are working in academia, you are part of a big community, you have colleagues, and so forth, so you can't afford to make too many enemies. People remain in place and if you antagonize a colleague of yours, you can be sure that sooner or later you'll meet him or her again on another committee. But when you are an independent scholar, you can more easily afford to make enemies. I think that's also part of the reason why we in the Freud field wage so many wars. Freud scholars are less civilized because they are not part of a big organization, of a bureaucracy.

MB-J/SS: You just commented on the attraction that Freud studies exert on people with a potentially unbalanced temperament and, indeed, you've actually written an article of February 18, 1989, entitled, provocatively enough, "On the Psychopathology of Freud Scholars." Are these people mad?

HI: I wrote this article for a daily journal, *Het Parool*, and I am not responsible for the title they gave to it. The article was about the hate campaign launched by Peter Swales against Peter Gay—

MB-J/SS: What hate campaign was this?

HI: Well, you know, when Swales tried to destroy Peter Gay.

MB-J/SS: As far as I understand it, Swales was uncovering a case of intellectual fraud involving the fabrication of history, in which Gay claimed to have discovered an important historical document that he had in fact made up. Isn't it somewhat tendentious to describe this as a hate campaign? You seem to move to the interpretation of motivations, exactly as the psychoanalysts. You said earlier that you were reacting against this attitude, but here you diagnose Swales's motivations, passing over the substantive issue of intellectual fraud.

HI: What you call intellectual fraud was one of the weapons used by Swales. But it was not his true motive.

MB-J/SS: How do you know his true motive? Are you his analyst?

HI: You're right. It's difficult to know the motives of people with any certainty. But don't forget, before this, there had been this huge conflict between Swales and Jeffrey Masson. Swales relished waging this war. In fact, I was myself a strong admirer of Swales, also of his campaign against Masson, partly because he did have a point there. Looking back, though, I tend to think that the campaign was very much exaggerated. But, again, it can't be denied that at the beginning Masson had done something very unfriendly, to say the least, to Swales. He had promised restricted research material from the Library of Congress to Swales in exchange for information on Fliess and, in the end, he didn't keep his promise. That's when Swales started his hate campaign. I was especially impressed by this hate campaign because until then I had only known academic life. Feelings of hatred also exist in academia, of course, but academics never launch campaigns like this. It was fascinating to see how this campaign was being conducted. Swales would later claim that Masson's fall was [Swales's] own making, but that is not so. Masson would have fallen out with the psychoanalysts anyway, with or without any campaign by Swales. But then Swales launched a new campaign against Peter Gay. Now, I think everybody must agree that Gay's [1988] biography of Freud is by far the best one we have got until now. Before that, there was only the Jones [1953–1957] biography, which is excellent but is still very tendentious. Gay's biography is much less tendentious and has less mistakes in it.

MB-J/SS: Many Freud scholars would argue the complete opposite, that in fact Gay is even more tendentious than Jones and that he introduces new errors into the literature.

HI: Every book introduces new errors. But Gay has far fewer errors and is much less tendentious than Jones.

MB-J/SS: I'll give you an example. In 1912, Jones has Jung going over to America to Fordham University to deliver what became *Transformation and Symbols of the Libido* [1911–1912]. This is the first time anyone made this claim, for Jung did nothing of the sort; he delivered his lectures on the *Theory of Psychoanalysis* [1913], a fact that is perfectly recorded in Jones and every other commentator. Why would Gay come up with something like that?

HI: I'm not going to argue with you about this. I am not a Jung scholar and here I am talking to a leading authority [i.e., Shamdasani] on Jung. So I assume that you're right when you say that this is a new mistake introduced by Gay into the literature. But what I am saying is that there are many more mistakes in Jones than in Gay. Just try to compare the number of mistakes in Jones and in Gay: I am prepared to make a bet with you that anybody who is not all too prejudiced will immediately come to the conclusion that Gay is more reliable than Jones.

MB-J/SS: I would like to go back for a moment to the issue of the psychopathology of Freud scholarship. We all agree that this field is pathogenic, but why is it so?

HI: Well, I just suggested two possible answers to that question. The first one is that psychoanalysis attracts people who are a little nuts. The other one is that most of these researchers are independent, so they don't feel the pressure of civilized behavior that is necessary to survive within a university.

MB-J/SS: You seem to be the spokesman in this affair of what Lacan used to call academic discourse, as opposed to analytic discourse.

HI: The animosity, the frauds, the threats are certainly unpleasant, but at the same time there is also something very attractive about this field. Freud scholars are much more outspoken, much less hypocritical than most people in academia. When I met Swales in the early 1980s, I was impressed by the level of his scholarship, but also by his fanaticism, by how deadly serious he was about his research. I had never encountered anything like this in the university. Here was a field in which people were personally involved, far more than in the academic world that I had known so far. This fanaticism is part of the field and it accounts for its emotional aspect, which can at times be so unpleasant. So, even while pleading for more civilized behavior in Freud studies, I have to admit that there is something very appealing about the authenticity that lies behind all this violence.

MB-J/SS: From being a Schreber scholar, how did you become a Freud scholar?

HI: During my research on Schreber, I had visited Morton Schatzman. He was at that moment deep in the last stage of his book *The Story of Ruth* [1980] and he obviously didn't have time to waste with a graduate student like me. At the time, I found him to be an unpleasant and arrogant fellow. I met him again in the early 1980s, after my dissertation had been published and translated into English. Schatzman liked my description of his treatment at the hands of the psychoanalysts, so we met again. This time, I encountered a different Schatzman, somebody I learned to like and admire. Schatzman had taken it on himself to send my dissertation on Schreber to Swales, so one day I received in the mail an offprint from this Peter J. Swales, whose name I didn't even know at the time, with a short note saying that he had an American publisher for me. Of course, it's always pleasant to get such a note from New York, so we started a correspondence and finally met. We did a lot of things together and it was through him that I was introduced into this whole field of Freud scholarship. This field seemed so terribly interesting that I soon decided to spend the rest of my life doing Freud research. Now I know better, of course. This field is also very unpleasant and, quite frankly, I think it's dangerous to spend your whole life there. A few decades, OK, but not your whole life! It's too unhealthy.

MB-J/SS: So what you are saying is that you got interested in Freud research through personal relationships rather than through an interest in Freud himself.

HI: That's right. The offprint Swales had sent me was a piece he had published on Freud and Fliess, in which he claimed that Fliess seriously thought that Freud wanted to kill him [see Swales 1989]. It was a nice piece of research, maybe a little too speculative, but nevertheless very well done. I was not interested in Freud; I was interested in this fascinating field of research.

MB-J/SS: So your interest in the history of psychoanalysis is an interest in the way people write the history of psychoanalysis rather than in psychoanalysis as such?

HI: Quite frankly, I don't know whether there is any difference between these two things. Why am I interested in all this? It's always hard to tell why you do things, but maybe I could say this: I'm interested in knowing how, for God's sake, such a curious doctrine as psychoanalysis managed to exert such an enormous influence on twentieth-century intellectuals. Now, is this an interest in psychoanalysis itself or an interest in what has been written about psychoanalysis? I don't know. Psychoanalysis is nothing else but books, articles, journals, congresses.

MB-J/SS: I would like now to move on to some areas of your Freud research. You've recently published in collaboration with Morton Schatzman [1993] a major article on "The Seduction Theory," in which you focus in particular on how Freud came to abandon the seduction theory. How, in your view, did this come about?

HI: As I am sure you know, this whole issue has become very controversial since the publication of Masson's *The Assault on Truth: Freud's Suppression of the Seduction Theory* [1984]. Indeed, Freud used to claim that he had been mistaken in 1896, when he believed hysterical patients who told him about having been sexually abused or seduced in early childhood; he had been naive enough to think that he had found the cause of their hysteria, until the moment when he realized that these stories were the reflection of the fantasy life of hysterics. Masson, on the contrary, claims that the seduction theory had not been a mistake at all: Freud should have continued to believe his female patients, as he had courageously done to begin with, instead of casting doubt on their stories of sexual abuse. So this is the controversy and it is absolutely groundless. Of course, I'm not the first to say this. Frank Cioffi already noted in the early 1970s that Freud's female patients never told him about sexual abuse in early childhood. If you look at the articles published by Freud in 1896, you'll see that Freud never writes, "Ladies and Gentlemen, here are a few more patients who tell me these stories; I believe them and this is the cause of hysteria." What he wrote is something quite different. He tells us that he had hysterical patients who didn't know anything about the causes of their illness and in particular didn't remember having been sexually abused in their early childhood. Indeed, Freud's theory was that if patients remember the seduction that took place in early childhood, they will in some way be protected against hysteria; it is only when they don't remember having been sexually abused that they fall ill. Freud keeps saying in these articles of 1896 that he tried to press his patients to confess that they had been sexually abused in early childhood, but that they wouldn't remember anything and that even after the treatment, they would still refuse to do so. He never says that patients came to him and told him about sexual abuse—quite the contrary, since it would have gone against his own theory! His seduction theory of 1896 was actually quite different from the description he gave later on.

Now, there would be much to say about the reasons why Freud felt compelled to "rewrite" the whole story, but the point is that the current controversy around the seduction theory is based on the description that he gave later on. Masson's argument still depends on the myth that Freud created about the seduction theory. But the actual seduction theory is not the one that everybody is talking about. Just read the texts, as naively as possible, and you'll see that things are different from what Freud would claim later on. Freud didn't begin to doubt the stories of his patients, simply because there were no such stories in the first place! So what happened is not that Freud abandoned his seduction theory by lack of courage, as Masson would have it. What happened is actually quite different. Freud initially thought that he had discovered the true cause of hysteria and that he would be able to cure his patients by uncovering their unconscious memories of sexual abuse in early childhood. He was so convinced of that that he didn't hesitate to boast in writing about therapeutic successes that he had not yet materialized. Now, in his private letters to Fliess, he writes repeatedly that he is trying very hard to achieve a therapeutic result with his patients, but that he hasn't succeeded yet. He comes back to this again and again, until he finally admits, in the fall of 1897, that he no longer believes in his theory. And the first reason he gives for this reversal is that he has not been able to finish "a single analysis" [*eine Analyse*] [Freud and Fliess, 1985]. So you see, the explanation is surprisingly simple; there's nothing mysterious about it. It's just that Freud had an idea and it didn't work. He tried very hard to make it work, but it didn't. So he decided to abandon it. It's as simple as that.

MB-J/SS: What is amazing about your demonstration is that it is so easy. You just need to read the texts.

HI: Yes, but I'm pretty sure that what we have written will not have any influence whatsoever on the current discussion about the seduction theory, for this is what has happened ever since Cioffi published his first article on this question. Cioffi is not the only one who has said that the seduction theory was quite different from the one discussed by Jeffrey Masson and the analysts.

MB-J/SS: Who else said that?

HI: Malcolm MacMillan [1997], for instance. It has also been demonstrated very nicely and convincingly by Jean Schimek [1987] a few years ago—but this article hasn't had any influence on the discussion, even though it was published in a psychoanalytic journal. People still want to see Freud either as a hero or as a villain, while in fact he was just an ambitious fellow who made stupid mistakes.

MB-J/SS: In your article you draw attention to a very interesting document discovered by Masson and published by him in his edition of the Freud-Fliess letters [see Masson 1985, 413]. It is a passage in a book published in 1899 by Leopold Löwenfeld, in which Löwenfeld claims that one of Freud's former patients told him that the scenes of seduction unearthed during his analysis were "pure fantasy." What do you make of this episode? Do you agree with Löwenfeld that Freud suggested the memories of abuse to his patients? Such a hypothesis would obviously move us away from the current debate about whether these scenes of seduction were real or fantasized.

HI: Yes, that's a wrong polarity and it is Löwenfeld who is right, of course. But you have to understand that Löwenfeld presents this case as an illustration of Freud's theory, not in order to contradict it. As I just said, Freud wrote that the patients didn't have any memories of sexual abuse and that he pressed them to "reproduce" these scenes. We don't know exactly what he meant by that, but it is likely that he forced them to do or to say certain things. Anyway, the patients would still deny that these were real memories, and this is Löwenfeld's point; Freud, he says, pressed these memories upon his patients, and [Löwenfeld] mentioned the case of the man who claimed that his memories of abuse were Freud's making. Freud would have had to agree on this point with Löwenfeld, since he himself stressed the fact that these were unconscious memories.

MB-J/SS: Yes, but he wouldn't have agreed with the implication of Löwenfeld's statements, namely, that these so-called memories were the result of suggestion on his part. Here is what Löwenfeld wrote (note that Masson doesn't quote this passage in the 1992 edition of his book): "The patients [in analysis with Freud] were subjected to a suggestive influence coming from the person who analyzed them, by which the rise of the mentioned scenes was brought quite close to their imagination" [Löwenfeld 1899, 195, 196].

HI: No, Freud wouldn't agree with that, of course. He would say that this was just another stupid patient who didn't realize how brilliant his discovery of unconscious memories was. But it is quite obvious that these memories were suggested by Freud. In my opinion, anybody who is interested in sexual abuse and its effects on the psyche should study present-day cases of sexual assaults and just forget about Freud's seduction theory. It only confuses the whole discussion to drag Freud into it.

MB-J/SS: Would you say that the value of your work is helping people to forget Freud?

HI: In this case, yes. I think the whole discussion about sexual abuse would have been much better off if people had said, once and for all, "OK, let's forget about this damn seduction theory." Certainly, this would have been a very positive thing. But I didn't do my research because I wanted to make people realize that. I did it because I just wanted to see what had happened.

MB-J/SS: In your paper, you draw out the significant series of false therapeutic claims made by Freud at the time: first the cocaine episode with Fleischl von Marxow, then the alleged cure of Anna O., and finally the eighteen cases mentioned in "The Aetiology of Hysteria" [1896]. What is the significance of these false therapeutic claims or mistakes Freud made? In your estimation, do they set the pattern for later psychoanalysis?

HI: No, because I think Freud made truly false therapeutic claims only in the early part of his career. At the time, Freud wanted to achieve fame by discovering some kind of new therapy. He started first with cocaine, then with hypnosis, and each time he published articles in which he boasted about therapeutic results that he had actually not achieved. This happened over and over again at the beginning of his career; he would be disappointed by a first "discovery," then make another one, publish therapeutic results which would turn out to be failures, then try something else, make new therapeutic claims, and so on. But that pattern, it seems to me, ended around 1900. What I am going to say now is somewhat speculative, but this is what I think happened. At the turn of the century, Freud went into some kind of a crisis when the seduction theory proved to be failure too, and I think he came out of this crisis a different man. Before 1900, Freud wanted desperately to cure his patients, because he saw therapeutic success as a proof of the correctness of his theories. After 1900, he seems to have decided that therapeutic results didn't matter so much after all. The reasoning was that if patients refused to get cured, this did not say anything negative about the theory, but only about the patient—who "resists," is "repressed," et cetera. Take the Dora case, for instance, which is the first major case that Freud published after 1900. You will see that Freud doesn't hesitate to present this case as a clear therapeutic failure. In a way, this was very honest, for people usually don't publicize their failures. But on the other hand, I have more respect for the Freud who still thought that he needed therapeutic results than for the Freud who simply assumed that if the patients didn't conform to his theory, then it was their fault. It seems to me that this was an easy way out of the problem that he had encountered earlier on: realizing that the therapeutic successes didn't come and not wanting to spend the rest of his life being disappointed, Freud simply decided that failures didn't matter any longer.

MB-J/SS: That's quite a charge concerning Freud's integrity, as least as a therapist.

HI: On the contrary. When Freud admits that Dora wasn't cured, this pleads in favor of his integrity. He hadn't said that about Fleischl von Marxow, whom he addicted to cocaine. He hadn't said that about Anna O., who ended in an asylum after Breuer's so-called cathartic cure. In the case of Dora, at least, he was very honest.

MB-J/SS: But what you are implying is that he was honest simply because he couldn't care less.

HI: Well, he no longer thought that therapeutic success was the decisive criterion for his scientific success. I hope I make myself clear.

MB-J/SS: Yes. What you're saying about Freud sounds very similar to Lacan's views on the problem of the analytic cure. Lacan would say that psychoanalysis has basically nothing to do with therapy and that curing the patients should not be the true objective of an analysis. The cure, according to him, is something that comes by chance or "in addition" [*par surcroît*] to the treatment. What do you make of this very honest theory of the cure, which is nowadays widespread in France?

HI: You know, I've tried several times to read Lacan, especially because Lacan has written so much about the Schreber case. I've tried to read him in French, I've read translations, I've read commentaries, but I've never been able to understand a word of it. What you just said is very interesting, but it is the first time that I hear something about Lacan that makes sense to me. I've always hesitated about whether Lacan was a pure swindler or something more than that. On the basis of his writings, I would tend to think that he is a pure swindler, but I also have good friends in France who have a tremendous admiration for him. Now, if what you're saying is true, this clearly shows that the man is a swindler. I mean, you ask people to pay a fortune to do therapy with you and at the same time you tell them that it doesn't make sense? This is a typical sign of what one might call a French disease of thinking. I presume that this is supposed to be funny, but science is a serious enterprise. What you quoted from Lacan is just a joke, a joke at the financial expense of people. This is something for which I don't have any sympathy at all.

MB-J/SS: I would like now to turn to the book you recently published called *The Freud Case*, which so far has been published in Dutch, German, and Spanish. Could you possibly summarize the general conception and argument of the book for English readers?

HI: I have tried to reconstruct what actually went on during the crucial period that came just before the beginning of psychoanalysis, the period of the early theories on hysteria. As I am sure you know, the stories about what happened during that time constitute an important part of the psychoanalytic folklore. They were created partly by Freud himself and partly by his followers, Jones being the most important among them. Since then, a lot of research has been done on these stories and it turns out that many things didn't happen like Freud said they did. Not only do these stories abound in factual mistakes, but they reflect a general tendency to rewrite the history of psychoanalysis along certain lines. For instance, Freud is presented as being much more isolated than he actually was, the work of his contemporaries on sexuality is systematically downplayed, et cetera. So a whole bunch of these stories have been shown to be mere legends. Nevertheless, nobody had tried so far to reconstruct the actual course of events, although it is not very difficult to figure out what really happened.

Take, for example, the collaboration with Josef Breuer. In later accounts, Freud would claim that although he and Breuer had discovered important things about hysteria, they had not yet realized at the time the importance of sexuality and that Breuer left out of prudery when he, Freud, started to emphasize it. This is Freud's own version of how he moved from the Breuer-Freud theory of hysteria to the next one, the famous seduction theory. But thanks to publications like Hirschmüller's [1989] book on Breuer, and Sulloway's [1979] book on Freud as a cryptobiologist, we know now that the importance of sexuality was already very much emphasized in his work with Breuer—and that Breuer wasn't reluctant at all to confront this aspect of hysteria. The question is, then, why did Freud feel the need to tell these lies about his collaboration with Breuer? Why did he say that he and Breuer had not paid attention to sexuality? I think I can give it an answer. Freud wanted to present his early theories of hysteria as a series of progressive steps towards psychoanalysis proper: first he discovered a few things together with Breuer, then he discovered the importance of sexuality, and finally he discovered the fantasy life of hysterics. Psychoanalysis could thus be presented as the result of a series of progresses. But the reality is quite different. Freud wanted to find a cure for hysteria and, together with Breuer, he thought that he had discovered such a cure. But, after having published the *Studies on Hysteria*, he quickly found out that he couldn't cure patients with this method. In fact, Freud says this with so many words in his article of 1896 on "The Aetiology of Hysteria": the cathartic method just didn't work, he tells us, and that's why he had to probe deeper and deeper into the history of his patients, until he arrived at events in the early childhood. The truth is that Freud gave up his first theory of hysteria because it didn't work, and then moved on to a second one. When this one didn't work either, he gave it up, too, and moved to a third one. So what Freud described later on as a series of progresses was in fact a series of failures. But Freud couldn't write that, of course, because then he would have had to admit that he had lied all along about the alleged therapeutic successes mentioned in the *Studies on Hysteria* and in his publications on the seduction theory. He had, therefore, to create a new story, and what he did is that he presented his early theories as more naive than they actually were. For example, he would downplay the role of sexuality in his work with Breuer in order to present his next attempt as being a progress, as the next step towards a better understanding of hysteria. So this is what my book is mainly about: I describe how and why Freud concocted a story that is quite different from what actually happened during this period, how and why he lied about his therapeutic results, how and why he gave misleading accounts of his early theories. I also deal in my book with the research Freud conducted on cocaine in the mid-1880s, when he was about thirty years old. During that period, Freud would already operate the same way, with the only difference that, being younger and more naive, he wouldn't cover his tracks as well. It was especially pleasant for me to write about this because I was lucky enough to get hold of transcripts of many of the letters Freud wrote to his fiancée, the famous *Brautbriefe,* most of which were still under restrictions imposed by Kurt Eissler.[1] In these letters, Freud would write at length about his friend and teacher Fleischl von Marxow, who was addicted to morphine and whom he had tried to cure with the help of cocaine. In several articles he published at the time [collected in Freud's *Cocaine Papers* in 1974], Freud presented this treatment as a major success, whereas in reality it was a major failure: Fleischl became severely addicted to the cocaine. Jones tells this story in his biography, but these letters to Martha Bernays give additional information about how Fleischl von Marxow's health deteriorated and what Freud actually witnessed while at the same time bragging publicly about this "successful" treatment.

MB-J/SS: So you are emphasizing, in your reading, the difference between Freud's original practice and his retrospective accounts. Likewise, you are stressing in the case of his work on hysteria, in which he claimed to have found a revolutionary new therapeutic method, no one would have

---

1. Most restricted Freud documents were finally made available to the public in 2000.

taken him seriously if he had said it arose out of a series of failures. In your view, do you see these fabrications and these legends as necessary for psychoanalysis as we now know it?

HI: Absolutely necessary. Psychoanalysis couldn't survive without these legends. Just think of it; Freud claims that the only way to judge psychoanalytic work is to undergo a training analysis, thereby becoming a pupil. This means that psychoanalysis is shielded against any inspection by outsiders. It's like a mystic experience. Let's say I have a mystic experience: you won't be able to know anything about it because it's something completely private. The only way for you to know whether what I am saying is true or not would be to undergo a mystic experience too. It's the same thing with psychoanalysis. But then, how come the lay public is so much impressed by psychoanalysis? It can't be because of psychoanalysis proper, since psychoanalysis, by its own account, cannot be assessed by people who have not undergone an analysis. So what is it that makes us believe that Freud is a great man and that psychoanalysis is such a fascinating field? It must have something to do with Freud's way of writing and his ability to create a narrative that appeals to everybody. All these legends about Freud's lonely quest for truth and about how his discoveries were rejected by everybody must appeal to something in ourselves. I mean, we are all lonely geniuses, right? Nobody acknowledges how brilliant we are, et cetera. I think the success of psychoanalysis is largely due to something like that.

MB-J/SS: That's quite a devastating estimation of psychoanalysis! Do you think that this legend has a future?

HI: Well, compare, for example, psychoanalysis to Christianity. As an intellectual system, psychoanalysis is much better structured, much more impressive than the Old and the New Testaments. And yet, Christianity has survived for thousands of years. So I don't know—psychoanalysis might have a future after all.

8

Suggestion, Hypnosis, and the Critique
of Psychoanalysis: Mikkel Borch-Jacobsen's
"Return to Delboeuf"

Interviewed by Todd Dufresne

Mikkel Borch-Jacobsen received his master's and doctoral degrees
in philosophy at the University of Strasbourg. In the mid-1970s Borch-
Jacobsen lectured in the Department of Psychoanalysis at the University of
Vincennes in Paris and in the Department of Psychology at the University
of Strasbourg. In 1987 he became a professor of French and comparative
literature at the University of Washington in Seattle.

Borch-Jacobsen's first book, *The Freudian Subject*, reflects his early
interest in psychoanalysis from a deconstructive perspective and is one
of the few important works in this field. That book was followed by a
biting genealogical work on French psychoanalyst Jacques Lacan, *Lacan:
The Absolute Master* (1991), and a collection of essays, *The Emotional Tie:
Psychoanalysis, Mimesis, and Affect* (1993). Borch-Jacobsen has, however,
grown wary of the poststructuralist interpretation of Freud, which he
claims is naively ahistorical. Consequently, his recent work has become
increasingly grounded in history, a change of emphasis largely facilitated
by a new appreciation of the role of hypnosis in the history of psychoanalysis. *Remembering Anna O.: A Century of Mystification* (1996) was designed
as a provocation on precisely this front and has taken a number of readers

by surprise. In it he establishes not only that the ur-patient of psychoanalysis, Bertha Pappenheim ("Anna O."), was never cured by Josef Breuer but also that the case study is a cynical and even fraudulent attempt to manipulate the facts. Borch-Jacobsen has also written dozens of articles, reviews, and newspaper commentaries, and has edited many projects, including coediting the controversial 880-page best seller, *The Black Book of Psychoanalysis: How to Live, Think and Get on Better Without Freud* (see Meyer, 2005), for French audiences. His latest books include *Folies à plusieurs: De l'hystérie à la dépression* (2002) and, in collaboration with Sonu Shamdasani, *Le dossier Freud: Enquête sur l'histoire de la psychanalyse* (2006).

The interview took place in my Toronto apartment in March 1997, one day after Borch-Jacobsen delivered a public lecture on the subject of trauma at the University of Toronto.

. . .

TD: You have for many years been interested in the role of hypnosis and suggestion in psychoanalysis. How does the "enigma of suggestion," as Freud called it, problematize research in psychoanalysis?

MB-J: As is well known, Freud was very scornful of the concept of suggestion. If suggestion is supposed to explain everything, he objected, then what is it that explains suggestion? One can agree with that, for it is undeniably true that suggestion is a very vague and ill-defined concept. Read the two books on suggestion that Hippolyte Bernheim published in the 1880s, and you will quickly realize that his notion of suggestion is based on an outdated nineteenth-century "physiology of the mind"—as Henry Maudsley put it in his book by that name—according to which ideas, when they are not inhibited and controlled by the superior functions of the brain, tend to be acted out automatically, without the help of consciousness. Suggestion, in this sense, is nothing else but a psychical reflex, the psychological equivalent of a knee-jerk reaction. Of course, that is not a very satisfactory explanation—at least for us.

But let's forget, for the moment, Bernheim's own theorization of suggestion. Taken in a nontechnical way, suggestion is a very simple idea—an idea that points to a problem, rather than to a solution. It means simply that all human interactions are, precisely, interactions: others react to what we are saying or doing, which is to say that we inevitably influence them. One of the implications of this very basic phenomenon is that we never observe human affairs from the outside, for we are always participants in what we describe. In this respect, I think Bernheim—and even more the Belgian mathematician, philosopher, and hypnotist Joseph Delboeuf, his friend and colleague—was right on target at the very beginning of so-called experimental psychology. Under the name "suggestion," they recognized something that later experimental psychologists have labeled the "experimenter's effect"—namely, that as much as we try to control experiments, our expectations will always influence, or contaminate, the results. Robert Rosenthal [1966] described the experimenter's effect in the 1960s, and as you may know, it has since become a huge problem in experimental psychology, a ghost in the machine that they can't exorcise.

Now, Bernheim's and Delboeuf's "suggestion" is nothing else but a name for this inevitable effect that affects all human interaction. So I think that it is not fair to say, as Freud does, that suggestion is just the name for a mystery. It may very well be a name for a mystery, but it is a problem in psychology that should be recognized and examined even before we attempt an answer.

TD: So what are the implications of suggestion for psychoanalysis?

MB-J: The implications of suggestion are obviously no less devastating for psychoanalysis—and, more generally, for what the historian Henri Ellenberger called dynamic psychiatry—than for experimental psychology. If even the most sophisticated experimental designs cannot prevent the experimenter's expectations and demands from contaminating the results, then what should we say about the highly "transferential" relationship between analysand and analyst? Obviously, the analysand is going to provide the analyst with all the confirmations that he is looking for. The French psychoanalyst François Roustang [1983] made that point some twenty years ago, and I don't see how one can dispute his argument. In this regard, it is no accident that Freud was so adamant about distinguishing the analytic manipulation of transference from suggestion. As he clearly recognized in the twenty-seventh of his *Introductory Lectures on Psychoanalysis* [1916-1917], if the transference elicits suggestive effects, then how can we be sure that the so-called findings [*Funde*] of psychoanalysis are not simply artifacts of the analytic situation? The fact is, we cannot, as I tried to argue in my 1985 essay on "Hypnosis in Psychoanalysis" [in Borch-Jacobsen 1993]. Incidentally, Adolf Grünbaum, whose work I didn't know at the time, had already made the same point in his *The*

Foundations of Psychoanalysis [1984]. Repression, the unconscious, Oedipal fantasies, infantile sexuality, the transference—these are not objective phenomena, nor are they concepts based on the careful observation of clinical data. They are the product of the analytic setup, of the analyst's interpretive strategies, of his theoretical expectations, and of the patients' eagerness to match these expectations. Freud's disclaimers notwithstanding, psychoanalysis produces, or "suggests," the evidence on which it rests. And that is why it is so difficult to refute: it acts as a perpetual self-fulfilling prophecy.

TD: If suggestion is the central problem of social relations, should it not also be the central problem of the human sciences in general?

MB-J: I think it should, although we might want to find a better name for it than *suggestion*. Clearly, it is not only psychology—clinical or experimental—that is affected by these looping effects. As is well known, the anthropologist's gaze disturbs or even destroys the cultures that he or she studies. Theories developed by sociologists, economists, or political scientists affect, in turn, the phenomena they are describing. The historian re-creates and changes the past on the basis of present concerns, and in the process changes the way we see ourselves. Et cetera, et cetera. All of this certainly calls into question the very notion of a social *science*. Indeed, we should go back to good old Delboeuf and take what he had to say seriously. He was certainly perceptive.

TD: What did you mean, the other day, when you told me you consider yourself a follower of Delboeuf?

MB-J: I said that somewhat tongue in cheek. But it is true that I take quite seriously the epistemological implications of what Delboeuf says about suggestion in hypnosis. You see, Delboeuf wasn't just a hypnotist. He started as a philosopher of science—Bertrand Russell admired greatly his critique of the postulates of Euclidian geometry—and he was a very sophisticated thinker, a friend of Gabriel Tarde, William James, and Théodule Ribot. What I find especially compelling in Delboeuf is something you don't find in Bernheim. Bernheim is very good at showing how the experiments of other people, like those of Freud's "master," Jean-Martin Charcot, are flawed because they are contaminated by suggestion. But he seldom reflects on his own practice. Delboeuf, on the other hand, not only says that Charcot's experiments are flawed but constantly admits that his own results are based on his own assumptions. In effect, Delboeuf was able to do something that very few social scientists in general are willing or able to do, that is, reflect upon their own intervention with what is being described. It is obviously very difficult to consider, in advance, the effects of what you are saying or doing. So I find Delboeuf's sophisticated epistemological awareness very compelling.

Of course, it is no accident that this conception or idea came to people who were working with hypnosis. Indeed, hypnosis is almost a caricature of the experimenter's effect, based as it is on the overt influence of hypnotist on the hypnotized—and vice versa, as Delboeuf was quick to note. Many researchers, such as Charcot, Charles Richet, Pierre Janet, and Alfred Binet, were trying at the time to envisage a scientific, objective psychology, based on the experimental study of hypnosis. But Bernheim and Delboeuf were from the beginning able to see through this project and recognize that the findings of this "scientific" psychology were not by any means objective. The implications of this recognition were therefore much broader than hypnotism, for they encompassed the entire field of incipient psychology.

What is very striking in this respect, and this is not a well-known fact, is that both Bernheim and Delboeuf gradually abandoned the use of hypnosis around the 1890s, precisely because they acknowledged that hypnosis is itself an artifact, a product of suggestion. As they both stated very clearly, there is no such thing as hypnotism; hypnotism is just an effect of suggestion. And therefore, since there is nothing genuine about hypnosis, they decided to do away with it and just use verbal suggestion. This was before Freud himself abandoned hypnosis as a psychotherapeutic technique. In fact, Freud had just jumped on the Bernheimian bandwagon, like many other psychotherapists at the time. I find it interesting that those who are portrayed by Freud as naive hypnotists were in fact the ones who saw through the hocus-pocus. And, actually, I find them methodologically and epistemologically much more sophisticated than Freud. Compared to them, Freud is a naive positivist. But, of course, if Freud had applied Delboeuf's methodological principles, we would never have heard of him.

TD: Do you believe that the problem of modern relativism began with the study of hypnotism?

MB-J: I wouldn't make any historical claim of that sort. But, in the realm of psychology, hypnosis as understood by Bernheim and Delboeuf was absolutely the beginning of this epistemological uncertainty. You find similar statements in William James's *Principles of Psychology*, but James had read Bernheim and Delboeuf.

TD: Can you tell me about your own experience with either psycho-analysis or hypnotherapy?

MB-J: Thank God, I have had no experience whatsoever with psycho-analysis! I already had serious reservations when the question of a personal analysis arose in the early 1970s. Those were the heydays of post–May 1968 Lacanianism in France, and I could see how friends of mine were totally swallowed up by analysis, quickly becoming blind devotees to the Cause. So I decided not to follow that path, and I'm glad that I didn't. Had I done so, I would probably be just another Lacanian clone today. Similarly, I was never in hypnotherapy proper. However, as I was interested in knowing how hypnotism works, I attended training seminars in hypnotherapy and, since training involves being hypnotized, had an experience with hypnosis.

TD: This is in the 1990s?

MB-J: Yes, in the early 1990s in the States.

TD: Why did you wait so long to investigate hypnosis in this manner?

MB-J: My good friend François Roustang urged me in this direction in the mid-1980s, but I never got around to it. I'm sorry about that, because I learned so much in just a few sessions. Many, many things became obvi-ous to me.

TD: Really? How did your experience with hypnosis alter your views on psychoanalysis?

MB-J: It's really very simple. Until then I still harbored a belief in what Freud called the unconscious. Of course, I didn't think of the uncon-scious in the same way as Freud.

TD: So you had already published three books on psychoanaly-sis, and then you had this experience with hypnosis which subsequently undermined your past beliefs in the existence of the unconscious!

MB-J: [laughing] You make it sound as though I underwent some kind of religious conversion! I see it rather as a theoretical sobering up. The experience with hypnosis made me realize that some of my assumptions were quite simply off the mark, and, rather than theorizing this experience away, as I could have easily done, I decided to revise my theory. What hyp-nosis taught me is really very simple: in hypnosis you are never "uncon-scious." On the contrary, you remain perfectly aware of what is happening. It's a kind of game you play with the hypnotist. Either you accept the game, or you don't. If you don't, then there is no hypnosis. But hypnosis itself is nothing but the acceptance, the very conscious acceptance, of the rules of the game called hypnosis, which may typically include the pretense of unconsciousness, of posthypnotic amnesia, and the like. Unconsciousness and forgetting—what Freud would later call repression—are just artifacts of the hypnotic game, a suggestion, as Bernheim and Delboeuf had clearly recognized one century ago.

Now, I knew very well that the notion of the unconscious came, historically speaking, from nineteenth-century theories of hypnosis. This is Ellenberger's great thesis in *The Discovery of the Unconscious*, and I agree with it totally. Our [Freudian] concept of the unconscious stems from Mesmeric double consciousness and, more directly, from Charcot's and Janet's investigations into hypnotic dissociation and the subconscious. That is not to say that Freud's unconscious can be simply equated with these first elaborations. But it is quite clear that the very idea of an unconscious psychical activity stems from the experience of hypnosis and of dissociative states, as Freud himself acknowledged on several occasions. Well, you just need to be hypnotized yourself to realize that this idea of an unconscious is rubbish. As I said, you remain perfectly aware of everything, even though the name of the game is to act as if you didn't. And, of course, once you realize that, you are bound to call into question all the theories that have been built on this illusion, the most notable of which is psychoanalysis.

I need, though, to preface what I have been saying in a Delboeufian way and admit that I studied a form of hypnosis propounded by Milton Erikson. Eriksonian hypnosis is based precisely on the idea that hypnosis is not a well-defined state and that we achieve hypnotic effects in the waking state. Eriksonians are not interested in promoting a deep state of hypnosis. With this in mind, I admit that my views about the unconscious may derive from my own theoretical bias, which is based on this particular experience with hypnosis.

TD: To the extent that Ellenberger legitimized the history of dissociated [altered, split] states in his history of dynamic psychiatry, did he not also open the door to the modern plague of multiple personality disorder [MPD]?

MB-J: Although Ellenberger's historical legitimization of nineteenth-century hypnotic theory, and of diagnostic categories like MPD, received an icy reception from orthodox psychoanalysts, it has been very influential in other quarters. His research certainly had a tremendous impact on young psychiatrists in the mid-1970s. As Ian Hacking has noted, MPD advocates, such as Frank Putnam and Richard Kluft, studied Ellenberger and regularly cite his work. And so, yes, I regret to say that this fine and decent scholar, whom I admire immensely, was probably part of this witch's brew that led to the recovered memory phase in North American psychiatry. Here we have another example of looping effect in the human sciences, in that Ellenberger's historical reconstruction contributed to the revival of the phenomena he was describing.

TD: Did Ellenberger himself believe in the dissociative phenomena that he was describing historically?

MB-J: I think he did, although it's hard to say for sure. He always tried to keep a safe, if illusory, distance from his subject matter, the distance appropriate to an objective historian. But obviously there is, behind this facade, a theoretical agenda for writing a book on the prehistory of psychoanalysis. He didn't produce this work for nothing. He wanted to relativize psychoanalysis, demonstrate that it was the tip of the hypnotic iceberg, and encourage us to read people like Pierre Janet more carefully.

TD: Ellenberger didn't want to establish the social construction of disease?

MB-J: No, I don't think so. Ellenberger had an implicit theory of the creative unconscious, not unlike Théodore Flournoy and Frederic Myers [investigators of spiritualism], which allowed him to see psychoanalysis as a derivative tradition. From a historical perspective, he was quite right. At the same time, he was certainly not a Delboeufian skeptic. Since I was so deeply influenced by Ellenberger, I, too, maintained a belief in the unconscious. Until, that is, I actually practiced hypnosis.

TD: So you were familiar with Ellenberger before you left for the United States?

MB-J: Oh yes. I read Ellenberger shortly after his book first appeared in French—in 1974, I believe—and it was a tremendous shock. I certainly think that his book is what put all of my own work in motion.

TD: And the work of an entire generation of French readers?

MB-J: No, for me in particular. Frankly, nobody read Ellenberger in France. Even my friend Léon Chertok, a distinguished historian of psychoanalysis and specialist in hypnosis, rarely mentioned *The Discovery of the Unconscious*. Although he knew Ellenberger very well and actually corresponded with him, Chertok didn't acknowledge the importance of this book. The same holds for Roustang, in spite of his interest in hypnosis. I was one of the very few who took this work seriously in France at that time.

TD: That's interesting, since this old interest in Ellenberger seems more consonant with your recent work, rather than with your early, more deconstructive works.

MB-J: You know, strangely enough, I think Ellenberger gave me the courage to do my deconstructive work. Granted, it's not readily apparent because I didn't engage in historical research in my early work. In this respect I was a typical deconstructionist who produced close textual analyses of Freud's work. Nevertheless, my interest in hypnosis came directly from Ellenberger. It is because I knew, from Ellenberger's historical work, that psychoanalysis was just the tip of the hypnotic iceberg that I allowed myself to be critical of Freud from the angle of hypnosis, suggestion, group psychology, and so on.

I should add that, while I was writing *The Freudian Subject*, I was translating into French with two friends all of Freud's early writings on hypnosis and hysteria, writings that were not available in French at the time. We intended to publish a critical edition of these texts, and we appended huge historical footnotes. To my mind, that critical edition was supposed to provide the historical counterpart of the theses that I had put forward in *The Freudian Subject*. Unfortunately, although these translations appeared separately in French journals, we were never able to obtain permission from the French copyright holders to publish a collected volume. In any case, this activity indicates that I was already doing historical work at the same time that I was writing *The Freudian Subject*. Since then, of course, history has become increasingly more important for my thinking. But history has always been in the background.

TD: What was your impression of American psychoanalysis before you left for the United States in 1986?

MB-J: I had no impression at all. Frankly, I was not very familiar with the Anglo-Saxon literature on Freud. I had a typical French, or perhaps European, prejudice against American psychoanalysis. Although I was already very critical of Lacan by this time, I was no doubt influenced by Lacan's own rejection of American psychoanalysis. So it was certainly an eye-opener when I began to read the Anglo-Saxon literature, which is rich with critical reassessments and primary source materials, such as oral histories.

TD: How important is oral history?

MB-J: Oral history is obviously very important for psychoanalysis. Kurt Eissler [1908–1999], a prominent analyst and founder of the Sigmund Freud Archives, understood that very well, and that is why he started systematically collecting interviews from Freud's patients and relatives from the early 1950s on. Unfortunately, he immediately put everything away under lock and key at the Library of Congress, so that the historian Paul Roazen [see Roazen 1975] had to do the same thing all over again ten or fifteen years later! Oral history is important if only because everything in psychoanalysis—at least, in principle—is based on clinical "observation." If we believe, for example, that young boys want to be sodomized by their fathers—what Freud called the negative Oedipus complex—or that women want to have babies to substitute for their missing penis, it is because Freud claims to have observed this in his practice. And since these observations were made behind the closed doors of Freud's office, we have, most of the time, no way of checking the accuracy of Freud's account of his analyses. We can only rely on Freud's word—which is precisely what psychoanalysts routinely do when they say that "psychoanalysis teaches us this . . . " or "psychoanalysis has proven that . . . " But if we are reluctant to trust Freud blindly, it is very important that we speak with the people who were involved in Freud's practice—whether it be his patients or, when that is no longer possible, with their relatives, their friends, et cetera—in order to compare their version of events with that of Freud. Roazen, Ellenberger, Peter Swales, Karin Obholzer, and other Freud sleuths have done precisely that, and what they have found, time and again, is that Freud's patients very often disagreed with his interpretations and that his case histories were highly selective and tendentious—if not, in some cases, downright misleading and fraudulent. One would never have been able to discern that without oral history.

That said, my only effort at oral history is the research I conducted with Peter J. Swales on the famous Sybil case. Thanks to the testimonies that we managed to gather, we were able to show that the founding case of MPD was based on misleading interpretations, a botched suggestive technique, and a rather opportunistic drive to cash in on a patient's condition [see Borch-Jacobsen 1997]. I think one could repeat this demonstration with most published case histories, for these problems are endemic in the field. Oral history is the Achilles heel of psychotherapy.

TD: Your French critics dismiss your recent work as American, by which I guess they mean revisionist.

MB-J: Isn't that amazing? Even the psychoanalyst René Major, whom I have known for almost twenty years and with whom I have shared many a bottle of French wine, called me an American academic in a lecture he gave on my Anna O. book! Of course, the French have a deep loathing for all things American—Disneyland, political correctness, the planetary domination of the English language, Coca-Cola, and Hollywood movies, et cetera—and so calling me an American becomes an easy way of rendering my work suspicious in the eyes of the public. In this way they can safely attribute my critique of psychoanalysis to my alleged puritanism, as Major proceeded to do, which was followed by the like-minded remarks of Freudo-Lacanian historian Elisabeth Roudinesco. At some point I'm probably going to be portrayed as a Christian fundamentalist or as a member of the militia!

My French critics also seem to think I have become a dumb positivist, a simpleton who believes in facts. They like to remind me that psychoanalysis is concerned with fiction and that nobody cares about the many scandalous details of its history. But they've got it all wrong. Far from being a positivist, I am a Delboeufian skeptic who believes that facts, in the human sciences, are always artifacts—constructs that result from complex interactions. The French have misunderstood my brand of revisionism and, since they are unwilling to listen, will continue to misunderstand. In fact, it is they who need to believe in facts, not me. It is they who need to believe, for example, that Anna O. was cured by Breuer or that Freud "discovered" the role of unconscious fantasies when he abandoned his seduction theory. They are sophisticated enough to realize that psychoanalysis is a theoretical fiction and that analytic practice is just an exchange of empty signifiers, a symbolic pact à la Lacan. But when it comes to Freud and the history of psychoanalysis, they are incredibly naive, if not ignorant. They are simply unable to see that the historical record is very damaging to Freud and to many of his clinical claims. That is why I am saying that I am less a positivist than my French critics: they still think there are "discoveries" in psychoanalysis; I, for one, doubt that there ever were such things as discoveries in psychoanalysis in the first place. In my view, these discoveries are all constructs, products, artifacts of the analytic setup.

TD: It is interesting to me that French poststructuralism as a movement has promoted that kind of ahistoricism, which is something it shares with structuralism.

MB-J: Absolutely. That is very apparent in Lacan. Lacan is the most dehistoricized, or acontextual, of all psychoanalysts. That Lacan removed psychoanalysis from any kind of validation, be it experimental or historical, helps account for the fact that the French are so immune to revisionist history. Thanks to Lacan, French psychoanalysis has become an entirely closed system: either you buy it, helter skelter, or you don't. It is not something open to revision or validation. In Lacan you not only don't find clinical validation, but you don't even find the *pretense* of clinical validation. Lacan very seldom mentioned his cases. He would say that "psychoanalytic practice tells us X," and then he would draw his theories; or he would say that "Freud tells us Y," and then he would draw his own interpretation of Freud's text. But there is absolutely no clinical or historical material upon which to ground these theories and interpretations. Lacan's psychoanalysis is, quite literally, a psychoanalysis without a patient—and without a history. Leaving aside the fascination that Lacan's theories and interpretations may hold for nonpsychoanalysts, I would reproach him for having banked on the authority of psychoanalytic experience while substituting for it an a priori philosophy of language and the subject inspired by G. W. F. Hegel, Alexandre Kojève, and Martin Heidegger. Lacanian psychoanalysis is, as you have argued for psychoanalysis in general, a bankrupt discourse, in the sense that it draws checks on a psychoanalytic experience that is simply nowhere to be found. And it will continue to do so as long as it can insulate itself and the public from the historical record.

TD: This is precisely why I am convinced by your unfashionable argument that psychoanalysis denies in advance the possibility of an outside from which to critique it [see Oakley 1997].

MB-J: Yes, you cannot critique psychoanalysis from the inside, as I once thought, because the inside is perpetually reconstructing itself. You will, for example, never be able to critique the notion of the unconscious from within psychoanalytic discourse. It is for this reason that the work of Freud historians, such as Ellenberger, Frank Sulloway, and others, is so important, for it allows one to go beyond the "closure" of its self-representation.

TD: I often hear fans of your early work express disappointment with the direction of your recent work, which is no longer deconstructive. The other day, an acquaintance, who happens to be a feminist theorist, spoke with regret about your recent book on Anna O., as though you had broken your arm or had suffered a breakdown.

MB-J: Well, you can tell her that I feel better, much better! You know, I think I am doing better theory now that I am more concerned with historical and empirical matters. That I don't speak about Hegel, Husserl, or Heidegger anymore doesn't mean that I am less theoretical. Quite the contrary, I am trying to sharpen my mind by confronting the facts. Again, I am not a die-hard positivist, obsessed with observation, verification, falsification, and so on; I don't believe in "hard" facts in the context of the social sciences, and I can very well live with epistemological uncertainty. But here is the crucial point: I am convinced that it is only when you consider the facts, *all* the available facts, that you can come up with a legitimate relativistic theory. If you gloss over the facts, or if you take them "ready-made," in a noncontextual way, you quickly end up with a dogmatic theory. So, again, I would say to my distinguished critics that *they* are the positivists, the true positivists, and the dogmatists. Theoretical sophistication is very often only a veil for a clandestine positivistic attitude.

TD: I sometimes get the impression that you regret your work will fuel even more work on psychoanalysis, one book piled precariously on top of the next.

MB-J: That's true.

TD: Has too much been written about psychoanalysis, and is silence an option?

MB-J: No, silence is not an option. But you are quite right: the more you critique psychoanalysis, the more you fuel psychoanalytic discourse. It really is a self-proliferating discourse.

TD: So do you regret your work on psychoanalysis?

MB-J: No, I don't. Absolutely not; that would be stupid. I don't disown anything.

TD: But do you wish you had studied something else?

MB-J: No, psychoanalysis is such a fascinating and exciting field! That is why I am still working on it, some twenty years later. It is just that I am a slow learner; it takes me some time to get things right. But when I get it right I nail it down. I realize now—and this is part of the reason I no longer recognize myself in my early work—that my earliest efforts were too decontextualized. I was a part of the French psychoanalytic culture I have just described, and I regret that. But that is where it happened.

TD: A few years ago, you mentioned to me that the time you spent studying Lacan was a waste of time.

MB-J: That sounds right. As a philosopher trained in Hegel, Husserl, Heidegger, Kojève, and so forth, Lacan's discourse seemed an old, albeit eccentric, discourse. So Lacan, quite unlike Freud, didn't teach me anything. For this reason, my book on Lacan is committed to showing how Lacan was just a derivative of all these other discourses. Perhaps other people will learn from me that Lacan was derivative in this sense—and rightly so, since it was for them that I wrote the book. But as for me, I didn't find anything new in Lacan when I finally found the key to his system. In this respect I feel a little cheated. Even so, I may have wasted my time, but now at least no one can throw Lacan in my face!

TD: Perhaps the most flippant response made in recent years to the critics of psychoanalysis has been the charge that they are mere "Freud bashers." This seems to be the same argument that has been thrown at critics from the beginning. So I ask: do you consider yourself a Freud basher?

MB-J: Everything is in the eye of the beholder. For psychoanalysts I am a Freud basher. But what does that mean? Freud bashing is a category that explains away critique by attributing it to the personal affects of the critic. As you say, it is what psychoanalysts have always done with critics. They claim that if we criticize Freud, it is because we resist his theory of sexuality, or because we are anti-Semites, or because we hate Freud. And don't think that this is old history. In 1997 Elisabeth Roudinesco actually gave a course on The Hate of Freud at the Ecole Pratique des Hautes Etudes in Paris. All critics of Freud since the beginnings of psychoanalysis were lumped together as Freud haters, together with Nazis and Stalinists. But again, what does that mean? The idea is that behind any critique of psychoanalysis—whether it be scientific, positivistic, philosophical, historical, or political—there is hate for Freud. That's ludicrous! We don't hate Freud. I certainly don't hate Freud, not any more than Lavoiser and Benjamin Franklin hated Mesmer or than Hegel hated phrenology. Actually, I sometimes find Freud quite clever, and I admire his theoretical and rhetorical chutzpah. But that's not the point. The point is not whether or not we like Freud, but whether or not his theoretical claims can be substantiated. So this whole "Freud bashing" business is absurd. We certainly don't go around calling orthodox Freudians "Freud lovers" or silly names like that, do we?

TD: Well, maybe just a little! [*laughter*]

9

Freud, Parasites, and the "Culture of Banality":
Todd Dufresne Speaks of Psychoanalysis
and Contemporary Theory

Interviewed by Antonio Greco

Todd Dufresne received his PhD in social and political thought at York University in Toronto, and is currently associate professor and chair of philosophy at Lakehead University. He is the editor of two books and the author of *Tales from the Freudian Crypt: The Death Drive in Text and Context* (2000) and *Killing Freud: Twentieth-Century Culture and the Death of Psychoanalysis* (2003). In *Tales*, Dufresne demystifies Freud's death drive theory of 1920—an idea routinely invoked, yet mangled, in the poststructuralist literature—placing it squarely in the tradition of Freud's earliest, least attractive, prepsychoanalytic metabiology. Dufresne also provides the linkage—almost universally ignored and misunderstood—between the death drive of *Beyond the Pleasure Principle* and the loving group psychology that followed in Freud's influential work of 1921, *Group Psychology and the Analysis of the Ego*. According to Dufresne, the death drive and the group psychology are really flip sides of the same coin; a coin whose currency is resignation and therapeutic pessimism, wild biological speculation, and the hating-loving politics of that apparatus-horde we call the psychoanalytic movement.

Dufresne met with Antonio Greco, a colleague and gestalt therapist, in Toronto over two days in November 1999, where they discussed at length

Freud and Freud criticism. The interview was reconstructed shortly afterward and then updated in September 2005 for inclusion in this book.

. . .

AG: How do psychoanalytic studies compare with academic work done in other fields?

TD: Very poorly. Frankly, in very few fields is the level of scholarship so slipshod. The blame for this problem can be traced to the fact that Freud and his close followers established psychoanalysis outside the university system by creating their own training institutes. For the goal of these institutes was less research and intellectual activity than the protection and transmission of doctrine from generation to generation. It was politics and religiosity, rather than ideas, that gave birth to institutional psychoanalysis in the 1920s.

Of course, this situation explains why analysts and their patients generally make for such lousy intellectuals, but it doesn't explain why intellectuals themselves have produced so many lousy books on psychoanalysis. It really is depressing to see how many bad books have been stamped, and will continue to be stamped, with the library code BF173.

AG: So the academics are not much better than the publishing analysts and their patients?

TD: Although there are exceptions, the field is overrun by advocates who have lost sight of anything resembling intellectual standards. In this respect, blind loyalty to psychoanalysis can often be correlated with the number of years someone has spent on the couch. For obviously it is hard to conclude, after significant emotional and financial investment, that psychoanalysis is groundless and, therefore, a waste of time. However, corruption comes in many forms and really can't be reduced to money and time spent with an analyst. In my line of work I am more disturbed by the corruption that accompanies the intellectual investment in psychoanalysis. Clearly you don't need to have been analyzed for years to become a zealous advocate on behalf of Freud and psychoanalysis. All you need to have done, depending on the size of your ego, is deliver a lecture or publish a book review, article, chapter, book or books, to become incapable of backing out of the enterprise. One goes public with one's ego and becomes incapable of retracting false beliefs.

AG: But surely these problems are found elsewhere in the university.

TD: You're right, of course. By definition, commentary in every field is parasitical and unavoidably requires a body of literature, a host, in which to set up shop. As such, it's easy to see how intellectuals discipline and order themselves. For without the host, the parasite dies; the insights of poststructuralism notwithstanding, "secondary" activities exist because we are willing to accept, at least contingently, that some other activities are primary. For this reason, parasitical intellectuals often establish cozy and conservative attitudes toward their host subject. In some cases, the intellectual even becomes an advocate on behalf of his or her field. And while this advocacy may or may not be justified given the social or political context, such advocacy has very little to do with scholarship.

But while this problem of corruption is present in all intellectual activity, it is rampant in Freud studies. To begin with, the central roles of fantasy and transference in psychoanalytic theory and practice seem to rationalize in advance the contamination of objectivity—and make it a routine cost of doing business. Thus do psychoanalysts laugh at the philosopher's naive belief in reality, since for them reality is merely a stage upon which we enact our subjective desires and fantasies. What is true for a Lacanian, for example, is quite simply this subjective appreciation of reality. So objectivity, including the problems of representation and correspondence, is left conveniently at the door of the analyst's office.

AG: What about the competing desires of the critics?

TD: I think too many critics are willing to play by the rules of this self-serving game, gullibly accepting the idea that their judgments can be—or should be—subject to the same belittling discourse that is applied to patients. Consequently, a critic might preemptively tone down his or her language, sprinkle flattery over a particularly damning conclusion, and make sure to promote Freud's genius at certain points in his or her argument. In short, the infected critic will police his or her conclusions in order to avoid the obvious charges of resistance, Oedipal-inspired parricide, negative transference, and so on. Other critics, typically those of a postmodernist bent, will accept that his or her subject position is "always already" entangled in Freudian discourse. And so the ideal of objectivity is abandoned even before the critique has begun—if it begins at all.

AG: How would you situate your own thought vis-à-vis that of other Freud critics?

TD: Well, in the most general sense my work wouldn't be possible without them. I am thinking of Mikkel Borch-Jacobsen and Frank Sullo-way in particular but also of people whose personal and intellectual cour-age inspired me, such as Paul Roazen and Frederick Crews. It wasn't easy, I think, for these pioneers to contest psychoanalytic ideas and institutions that almost everyone took for granted. Criticism can mean isolation, self-doubt, and even ridicule. But it can also mean principle, taking a just stand, and this is unfortunately very rare. It's always easier to go with the flow and to make nice with everyone. So, as a relative newcomer to the field, with less than fifteen good years into it, I owe these critics a lot intellectually and, I'd say, morally. So that's first off.

But on a deeper level you've asked a very difficult question, because Freud critics are by no means a homogeneous bunch. Moreover, there is an unsettled disagreement about truth and epistemology—unsettled because it is usually ignored—that divides the critics. On the one side are those critics, still in the minority, who find fault in psychoanalysis, and yet are predisposed toward Continental philosophy and also, to some degree, poststructuralism. These are people interested in discourse, Kan-tian-styled critique, and the limits and ethics of representation. Despite some reservations, I would include myself in this group—but personally think its most coherent exponent has been Borch-Jacobsen [see Chapter 8]. And this, I should add, despite the surface differences between Borch-Jacobsen's early deconstructive work and his later, more openly critical assessment of psychoanalysis, and, second, despite his own well-consid-ered reservations about French poststructuralism. The truth is that very few people with a poststructuralist background even care about criticism of Freud. But among those that do, I would argue that it makes a differ-ence. For example, it makes talk about discourse, fiction, and construction more likely.

On the other side are a far greater number of Freud critics, those who openly side with empiricism and science, or at least implicitly advocate the principles of reason and the Enlightenment, and see their critical engage-ment as part of that project. Whether they say so explicitly or not, their work is therefore aligned with analytic philosophy, which is to say, with Anglo-American philosophy. Sulloway is a significant figure of this per-spective, and his work is absolutely first rate.

AG: And Crews?

TD: I think Crews has come to stand in for Freud criticism more generally—at least in the eyes of the general public, where he is deservedly well known and respected. Like I said, I'm certainly a fan of his work. I agree with his critical assessment of Freud and psychoanalysis and have the greatest respect for what he has done for Freud criticism. Moreover, I am sympathetic to his stand on rationality, which he ties explicitly to the ideals of democracy. During an interview Crews basically told me that he wants to protect democratic principles from the kind of intellectual thuggery and hypocrisy that inevitably snuggle up to grand interpretive schemes like psychoanalysis. This makes sense to me. Consequently, and despite my retrograde attraction to some aspects of poststructuralism, the analytic rebel in me finds Crews's faith in reason and social justice attractive. I recognize that the indulgence of radical elements within democracy is itself a luxury afforded by democracy.

But for me the ideal of democracy is strengthened by a certain amount of what Nietzsche once called "illiberality to the point of malice."[1] In this vein I have a measured affection for many of the thugs and con artists that Crews finds morally and intellectually repulsive. For example, I am merely amused by the colossal absurdities of Freudo-Marxism. I also find the works of explicitly antidemocratic thinkers attractive, which, after all, include among their ranks recognizably great figures like Socrates and Nietzsche. My impish playfulness reflects a part of postmodernism that Crews rejects—the part he views, I would guess, as irrational and socially irresponsible. So, to put a fine point on it, while we are both happy gadflies attacking the established truths of psychoanalysis, my style or mood is quite different from his.

AG: So you reject science and empiricism, features associated with the majority of Freud criticism?

TD: Well, it doesn't follow that Continental-leaning thinkers are necessarily and simply antiscience. Obviously I agree that science and empiricism are essential mediums for acquiring a certain kind of knowledge about things. I like bridges that don't fall down and toilets that flush. But I approach these achievements much the same way I do democracy; that is, I embrace the critics of science and instrumental rationality as an essential and interesting part of the process. As a result I am, in principle,

---

1. Nietzsche writes: "In order that there may be institutions, there must be a kind of will, instinct, or imperative, which is anti-liberal to the point of malice." In Nietzsche 1888, no. 39.

favorably disposed to the undecidability of Jacques Derrida and Jean-François Lyotard and am attracted to the sorts of nominalism found in Michel Foucault and Nelson Goodman. It follows that I am also generally less interested in truth and reality than in truth effects and discourse. From this orientation follows my interest in historicizing the discourse of psychoanalysis. Well, why historicize? Because this mode reveals that psychoanalysis is in fact *not* a science, has little or nothing to do with truth, save for the truth we glean from a cautionary tale, and is really the institutionalization of one man's ambition, fantasy, and desire. As a consequence, I can easily agree with my science-oriented colleagues that psychoanalysis fails miserably according to the dictates of that discourse we call Western science. And I agree that this is an important and essential critique, especially in light of Freud's own thought and the desperate efforts of analysts and scholars who repeatedly try to extricate Freud from his own worst and most embarrassing mistakes. But once we agree that psychoanalysis is not a science, I think that we have to discuss just what it is and how it came to be mistaken as a science—beginning with Freud's own view of things. These are moral and political questions, broadly conceived, and I personally don't think the analytic mind-set gets us very far in thinking deeply about them.

That said, I am not an expert in the philosophy of science and reserve the right to change my mind! So who knows—Crews and the others may yet convince me to abandon my few remaining delusions. The important thing to remember is that the science-friendly Freud critics like Sulloway, and the Continental-inspired critics like Borch-Jacobsen, all agree that Freud's theories are *not* what he claimed they were, namely, empirically derived, objectively known discoveries and universal truths. Given Freud's own assumptions, all the critics can agree that he was a rotten scientist. But, again, as for why it is we do what we do, or what it is that motivates our sometimes similar-sounding analyses, I'm afraid there is something of the divide I've just sketched.

AG: Some complain that critics of Freud, regardless of epistemology, go too far and are merely advocates and polemicists for the opposing camp.

TD: It is true that I am in another camp than many, perhaps even the majority, of Freud scholars. But I would say that this is true for a very simple reason: they happen to be mostly wrong, while we are mostly right!

AG: I know you are joking, but doesn't this sort of statement prove the point that you aren't free from the corrupting effect of polemicizing? Among other things, I'm thinking of your [February 18, 2004] op-ed for the *L.A. Times*, "Psychoanalysis Is Dead . . . So How Does That Make You Feel?," which seemed needlessly provocative to me.

TD: Yes, that earned me lots of amusing hate mail—but also some kudos, too, so maybe things are looking up for the field. If it helps, Tony, it was my editor who created the title for that article. But, you know, I don't disown it, either. Look, I'm a big fan of clear and distinct, cool and restrained argumentation. But there is a time and a place for polemics. This reminds me of an amusing remark that Sandor Ferenczi once made to Freud. Let me read this passage from a letter of March 9, 1911: "As for polemicizing against opponents, I am entirely of your opinion. This kind of polemic is also boring and painful to me. And yet I also want to force myself to do it in the future" [Freud and Ferenczi 1993, 258]. So when is it a good time and place for polemics? Precisely after one has made a clear and distinct argument. The right to make a polemical remark has to be earned in order to be respected.

AG: But don't you deplore the polemics of your opponents?

TD: Yes and no. I respect anyone willing to argue a case with passion and wit. It is to Freud's credit as an artist that he was such a great writer and a clever polemicist on behalf of his beliefs. But the artist was fundamentally mistaken about many things, or, to put it more accurately, Freud's artistry always came before the facts. Clearly, Freud's admirable passion and wit are not always supported by rigorous argumentation. On the contrary, he was a romantic thinker who used reason to rationalize his mistaken, sometimes laughably mistaken, beliefs—from his metabiological fantasies to his psychoanalytic portraits of historical figures.

The same point holds for current debates in the field. Although it is often pointless and depressing, I am in principle still willing to argue about Freud with anyone, provided the humor isn't too malicious and the arguments aren't merely ad hominem. But I have no patience whatsoever with my colleagues who spin the facts to suit their arguments and who resort to adolescent name-calling to smear an opponent. As one of the original petitioners of the Library of Congress Freud exhibit [ca. mid-1990s], I can appreciate what it is like to be the victim of misinformation, lies, and hate. As a group we were called fascists, ayatollahs, censors, and so on [see Dufresne 2003, chapter 7]. Of course, this verdict is ironic since our advocacy was on behalf of openness and fairness. Moreover, we shared no political agenda in common and—let's be honest—don't necessarily know, like, or even respect one another. So these are the facts. But a certain brand of polemicist doesn't care one whit about facts. I am afraid that well-reasoned, clear, and distinct ideas are in too-little evidence in Freud studies. Consequently, the polemics are often undisciplined and personal, even among fellow travelers.

AG: Aren't clear and distinct ideas, a staple of Anglo-American philosophy, unsuited to someone influenced by poststructuralism?

TD: I have had that observation thrown in my face a number of times—typically, and I think tellingly, by angry graduate students with nothing to lose but time. Well, nowadays I take that observation as a compliment, backhanded or otherwise. Why? Quite simply because I now see much of poststructuralism as a handmaiden of psychoanalysis. And since I think psychoanalysis has been a terrible mistake, I cannot entirely approve of another theoretical movement that has advanced and continues to advance this mistaken agenda. Of course, I didn't recognize this complicity as a problem at first—and to be honest, I wasn't willing to recognize it. You need to have ears to hear such things, especially when you are young and trying to earn some interest on your hard-won intellectual investments.

AG: You are still young!

TD: Maybe so. But at one point in my graduate education I realized that it was just too easy to go along and ape the mind-set and, above all, the styles of various poststructuralists. So what began for me as an exciting project on the edge of traditional thinking quickly became dull and conventional. Nowadays I tend to think that clear and distinct ideas, no matter how boring they are, can often be the most radical way of proceeding. Of course, many of us have been trained to think that well-considered arguments and cold, hard truths are inherently violent, misogynistic, patriarchal, logocentric, and so on. But, again, this view, once adopted to criticize dominant ideologies, has become just another ideology. Worst of all, it has lent its intellectual authority and institutional prestige to the abuses of identity politics. But is it really acceptable that deviations from the party line result in a litany of abusive name-calling and blacklisting? Does our thinking have to be so policed and banal? Dare I say it, so "fascistic"—to throw it back at these critics? For me, this culture of banality, grown on the back of poststructuralist critiques of essentialism, has nothing to do with decent scholarship and everything to do with advocacy. I've certainly had enough of it.

AG: But can't we thank poststructuralism for challenging old preconceptions inherited from a father-knows-best philosophy?

TD: Sure we can. Poststructuralism began with a radical impulse to dismantle and reassess the philosophical tradition, beginning with a critique of the modernist subject inherited from Descartes. Scholars like Derrida and Foucault taught us how to read old texts differently, and we owe them a substantial debt. I do, in any case, and see them as an absolutely crucial part of the Continental tradition. But to keep churning out work in their style twenty-five years later has become a bore and, as it has become more acceptable within the university, merely another kind of convention. Moreover, because so much of poststructuralism has wedded itself to psychoanalysis, otherwise intelligent people have been incredibly slow to appreciate the importance of Freud criticism. Why? Because so much of this criticism, as I was just saying, is associated with analytic thinkers like Sulloway. I think poststructuralists have been part of a knee-jerk reaction that crudely prejudges Freud criticism as naive, positivistic, politically correct, and all-around distasteful—in a word, as American. Naturally, this prejudice has had serious implications for scholarship. For instance, seemingly sophisticated people simply avoid reading certain works of criticism or, if they do read them, studiously avoid acknowledging them. Or worse, they read the critics in order to misinterpret them—so that everyone else can then feel perfectly justified in ignoring them. In other words, I'd accuse poststructuralists of operating very much like the psychoanalysts did during the last century.

This is too bad, of course, since the first poststructuralists were obviously not following a rigid playbook of poststructuralism. Codification came later. In my opinion, we do these creative thinkers a disservice when we ignore their own most radical impulses—but so did they when they established themselves, or were established by others, as the latest in a line of gurus and prophets. We need fresh air to breathe, and I recommend using their theoretical sophistication against them, something I have attempted in my own work on the poststructuralist interpretation of Freud.

AG: In *Tales from the Freudian Crypt* you turn the proliferation of opinion about Freud's death drive theory to critical advantage. But what does this proliferation of opinion teach us about Freud's critics?

TD: I tried to make the heterogeneity of opinion about Freud's death drive theory work on a few levels, one being a pointed criticism of the arbitrary nature of criticism in the history of psychoanalysis. In this respect the apparent dissensus about the fundamentals of psychoanalysis is a scandal. For this dissensus implies that, for over one hundred years, smart people haven't been able to derive any conclusions about Freud's so-called discoveries, that the verdict is still out. But that's untrue! Informed critics know very well that Freud fabricated his findings and was motivated by factors other than science and objectivity.

So why do so few people know, or care to know, about these some-times stunning facts? In no small measure, and as you were just hinting, the pundits and critics themselves are to blame. In *Tales* I tried to expose the irreconcilable absurdity of Freud commentary over the last hundred years, from Reich and Marcuse to Lacan and Derrida. It's obviously not the case that these people are ignorant. It is rather the case that these crit-ics, like Freud before them, are motivated by special interests, for example, by Marxist, structuralist, or poststructuralist interests. And because their works are dogmatically blind to intractable problems in Freud's work, including basic facts, they have the effect of blinding nearly everyone who reads them. We love to be dazzled, even by the spectacle of crushed glass.

AG: But what is a "basic fact," and who is in a position to know one when he or she sees one? Isn't this where the postmodernist appreciation of Freud comes in?

TD: First of all, yes, the "posties"—postmodernists and poststruc-turalists—have generally embraced the idea that history is just a kind of fiction. I am sympathetic to this idea and am willing to entertain it up to a point. I have written about fiction and history in psychoanalysis pre-cisely because, given the preeminent role of fantasy in the field, one has a tough time distinguishing between fact and fiction, history and case study. I think this is an interesting and amusing state of affairs and have even included a biographical fiction in *Killing Freud* that is meant as a send-up of the kind of historical work that we all read and cite. But I attempt this work in an ironical spirit, believing that there are indeed facts, even if psy-choanalysis has made it seem near impossible for us to know them. This, then, is a problem for psychoanalysis—but not really for me.

Naturally, though, I do worry about being too cavalier about facts in history. Is it really the case that the opinion of, say, a Holocaust denier is equal to another who believes that three million Jews, rather than six million, were killed in concentration camps? One says it didn't happen at all, while another questions the interpretation of facts. I reject the idea that truth is relative at the level of basic facts, and to this extent echo something Borch-Jacobsen has said [see Chapter 8]; namely, any relativist who ignores the facts risks becoming a dogmatist. He's right. When posties say, for example, that the fabricated foundations of psychoanalysis don't matter—primarily, they claim, because psychoanalysis is only interested in fantasy—they are being absurd dogmatists.

But this response is still not entirely satisfactory, since it doesn't address your first two questions—namely, what is a basic fact, and how can we purport to know one? I would say, thinking of the historian R. G. Collingwood, that there are two kinds of history: one that barely deserves the name, as it was once practiced long ago, and modern history. The first is what Collingwood rightly calls scissor-and-paste history and is more or less concerned with recording dates, names, and events; for example, on the Ides of March, Caesar crossed the Rubicon. The second is interpretive history and is concerned with the interpretation of dates, names, and events; for example, on the Ides of March, Caesar crossed the Rubicon because he was a megalomaniac, or because he wanted to defeat his enemies, or because he was a compulsive bed wetter, and so on.

How does this distinction between basic and interpretive history help us? Well, because the majority of Freud scholarship, like modern history generally, is so obviously an interpretive history. The posties know this better than anyone and are, in my opinion, quite right to conclude that such interpretation, like analysis, is radically interminable. We can engage in debate about motives forever. However, there is a fundamental problem here in the case of psychoanalysis, since all historical interpretation, even the freewheeling interpretive history of postmodernists, is still based on the scissor-and-paste history of mere dates, names, and events. And this is where the posties drop the ball. For almost all of the best critiques of Freud made over the last thirty years—the kind I associate with the creation of "Critical Freud Studies"—have begun by examining basic facts about dates, names, and events.

What these critics have found is that the history of Freud interpretation is the history of misinterpretation of a fundamental kind; namely, it is interpretation of facts or events that *never happened*. For example, they have found that Freud, during the period of "discovery" and subsequent abandonment of the seduction theory, exaggerated his results and, when necessary, simply made them up.

AG: Freud said he crossed the Rubicon when he didn't?

TD: Worse. Not only didn't he cross the Rubicon, to extend the analogy, but it turns out in this case that the Rubicon itself doesn't exist! It's all a myth. And so, while the posties inevitably berate Cioffi, Crews, Sulloway, and others for their naive belief in facts, they have simply fallen into the rabbit hole that Freud dug for them. For his part, Borch-Jacobsen replies that it is really these naysayers who are being naive. I would only repeat my suspicion that our gullible colleagues have risked their egos on baseless interpretations that they are now incapable of retracting.

Of course, the stakes are now very high. For if the critics are right, then the majority of Freud interpretation is utterly worthless. And it is worthless in at least two ways: as history and as interpretation. At best, these groundless interpretations are a kind of literary garbage—works of unwitting fiction along the lines of medieval discussions of angels. It's true that these works tell us a lot about the beliefs of a certain period, in this case the twentieth century, but they don't work the way the authors intended them. To start with, they are not just untrue, they are delusional. Why delusional? Because a totally unverifiable and highly poetic discourse, founded by Freud, has been mistaken by others as actually true. And because of this fundamental mistake, all subsequent interpretations expounded on the basis of it are ever more ridiculous and absurd. So for me, again, they are best understood as cautionary tales—what Lacan would call "poubellications," or published trash.

AG: If empiricism is just a theory, isn't a basic fact just an interpretation among others?

TD: That is true and a little bit clever, but a degree of certainty is all I am after. I'm not saying that we can't get our basic facts wrong, which we obviously do. It is rather that we must be willing to revise our interpretations on the basis of the basic facts we do have. I don't entirely blame Freud scholars for making a mess of everything with their erroneous interpretations. Freud misled everyone, beginning with himself and his closest followers. Psychoanalysis is a con game, after all. That said, short of sticking our heads in the sand, we must confront the basic facts and rewrite the history of psychoanalysis anew. And that's just what good readers of Freud have been doing since the late 1960s.

AG: Unlike what you call the best criticism of recent years, you have leapt headfirst into the "interpretive garbage." Is this a significant shift in emphasis?

TD: For me it is. The best critics have pretty much milked the scissor-and-paste history of psychoanalysis—that is to say, they have largely corrected the basic facts about Freud. I mean, I'm sure that there are many more things to discover about the fabricated origins of psychoanalysis, but the foundation for an alternative understanding of psychoanalysis has now been laid. That's what we should do now, and what I have attempted. And, you're right, unlike most of my colleagues, I am fascinated and amused and disgusted by the interpretive garbage, something I say explicitly in the preface to *Tales*. I recount all this stuff as a kind of performance, in part to demonstrate the real "repetition compulsion" in psychoanalysis, and in part to exhaust and thus extinguish psychoanalysis under the weight of its own absurdity. One thus writes psychoanalysis to death by using its own detritus.

AG: And so the game of interpretation begins again!

TD: Yes, I'm afraid it does. But interpretation is a potentially valuable part of scholarship, so I'm not worried. In this respect, I like to remind my social scientist colleagues especially that primary documents and original research, while important, aren't everything. In fact, as Frank Cioffi points out [see Chapter 6], the field of psychoanalysis really doesn't need any more discoveries of primary materials. There are plenty of materials available and this has long been the case. What the field needs is thoughtful and informed readers capable of decoding and assessing meaning in light of the facts we know. And so, despite their poor record in the twentieth century, the field really does need literary critics and philosophers. But to be effective these scholars need to read work that goes against the grain of their own narrow disciplinary views and epistemological commitments.

AG: Do you consider *Tales from the Freudian Crypt* to be a "true" history of the death drive?

TD: There is more to say about Freud's late theories, including the death drive theory, but I think my contribution rings true. We can always argue about the bits and pieces. But it's plausible interpretive work because it's not blatantly false work. To begin with, I recognize facts that some others don't recognize at all—such as Freud's essential biologism. As I say in *Tales*, in relation to Derrida's work on Freud, any reading that fails to come to grips with Freud's fundamental biologism is quite simply a bad reading.

AG: Isn't there a danger that, having destroyed the accepted interpretations of psychoanalysis, you have also destroyed your own position as a critic? If it's all about "killing Freud," then aren't you the worst kind of parasite, namely, a parricide?

TD: On the one hand, you're right. I understand why people are uncomfortable with this sort of activity. To them, a virulent kind of criticism destroys everything, leaving nothing. To carry on with your metaphor, such criticism is considered a virus that kills its own hosts—which seems inherently stupid and self-defeating. I, however, see things quite differently. First of all, it is time we flipped the metaphor of host and parasite on its head. For as I argue in *Tales*, it is psychoanalysis that has lived off its critics—not the other way around. It is Freud, not the university, that has benefited the most from this relationship. As for the loaded claim that some critics are "killing" Freud, a line of attack forwarded by the Chicago philosopher Jonathon Lear, it is merely a melodramatic and entirely predictable way of diagnosing our supposed pathology without addressing the criticisms we have advanced. You know, we are fascists or politically correct "Americans" or troubled Freud bashers or whatever. To informed readers, however, it's all just business as usual.

As for the title of my book, *Killing Freud*, it was designed as an open provocation to the propagandists for Freud, most especially those who still utilize psychoanalysis as a weapon to destroy or demean their enemies. What I did, of course, was appropriate the accusation of parricide, wear it as a badge of honor, and throw it right back at our critics. In truth the book is just a collection of articles, some of them amusing and polemical, that attempt to justify in fairly accessible terms why it is that some of us cannot believe in the claims of psychoanalysis. Truth is a killer in this book—that is, a killer of that which is false. But the result is actually pretty mundane: at last Freud has been transformed into a proper object of historical and intellectual interest, a figure suitable for examination in the university.

AG: Freud studies have finally come of age?

TD: Freud scholars, in any case. The lost cause of psychoanalysis, so infused with a nonintellectual and even anti-intellectual bias, dominated by partisan interests, and characterized by a stunning degree of ill-will and prickish behavior, has finally made way for a new cause, actually an old one—that of rigorous, informed scholarship. That's why the death of this era should inspire a few years of celebration. We've certainly earned it.

Suggested Readings

Excellent secondary texts, many of them modern classics, include Henri Ellenberger's *The Discovery of the Unconscious: The History and Evolution of Dynamic Psychiatry*, originally published in English in 1970, and Paul Roazen's *Freud and His Followers* of 1975. Ellenberger's work is especially rich with information, anecdotal and essential, although far more than necessary for readers with a passing interest. Roazen's work is less expansive but much more accessible. He interviewed many people (unfortunately without recording them on tape) from the early history of psychoanalysis and makes numerous references to their thoughts. For a dramatic account of Freud's inner circle, see also Roazen's controversial book of 1969, *Brother Animal: The Story of Freud and Tausk*. It reads like a novel.

Philosopher Frank Cioffi and the historian of science Frank Sulloway are two more key figures of the 1970s. Cioffi's early essays, including the famous "Was Freud a Liar?" of 1973, were far-flung until collected in his sometimes tough-going but uniformly worthwhile *Freud and the Question of Pseudoscience* of 1998. Sulloway's great book of 1979, *Freud, Biologist of the Mind*, was received at the time as a bombshell. Many still don't agree with it, but mostly because they refuse to read it. His thesis, that Freud's work is informed by an outdated biology, has been very influential among informed critics of psychoanalysis. I recommend it highly, not just as excellent intellectual history but as an anecdote to decades of partisan histories of psychoanalytic theory.

Recommended works on the early history of psychoanalysis include Mikkel Borch-Jacobsen's *Remembering Anna O.: A Century of Mystification* (1996). In it he gathers all the available information, much of it shocking, to provide the best overall reconstruction of Josef Breuer's case of Anna O.—the ur-case of psychoanalysis. For the best work on Freud's pre-psychoanalytic seduction theory, the idea that hysteria is caused by childhood sexual abuse, see Borch-Jacobsen's essay, "Neurotica: Freud and the Seduction Theory" (1996), published in the journal *October*, and Cioffi's collected work of 1998. Consider also Allen Esterson's lesser known, but very helpful, *Seductive Mirage* (1993). Note that Cioffi is especially good at rebutting the arguments made famous by another critic of Freud's seduction theory, Jeffrey Masson, in *The Assault on Truth: Freud's Suppression of the Seduction Theory* (1984). Masson essentially accuses Freud of dropping the theory because he lacked the courage of his convictions. The critics I have just noted argue that Freud dropped it because it was a mistaken idea, based in part on his naïveté concerning suggestion, and that his turn to psychoanalysis was a sleight of hand designed to help him escape responsibility for his serious error. Finally, for a strong, comprehensive, although fairly dry, examination of the early history and theory of psychoanalysis, see *Freud Evaluated: The Completed Arc* by the retired Australian psychologist Malcolm Macmillan. Look for the corrected and expanded second edition of 1997.

For additional work on the theory of psychoanalysis, see the philosopher Adolf Grünbaum's *The Foundations of Psychoanalysis* (1984). In this fairly advanced work he finds the validity of clinical evidence in psychoanalysis to be sorely lacking. Borch-Jacobsen's *The Freudian Subject* (1988) is good at teasing out complex arguments and contradictions concerning identity and identification. But as he now admits, although his early work is implicitly critical of Freud, it does not openly draw negative conclusions. That comes later. François Roustang's *Psychoanalysis Never Lets Go* (1983) is a more accessible but still sophisticated reading of Freud's ideas. See, in particular, his very smart chapters on suggestion and transference. My own *Tales from the Freudian Crypt: The Death Drive in Text and Context* (2000) is at least as accessible as Roustang's book. In it I provide the only book-length discussion about the meaning and reception of Freud's late theory of the death drive, announced in 1920. By focusing on the death drive theory, I provide a useful way to learn something about such Freudians as Sandor Ferenczi, Melanie Klein, Jacques Lacan, Herbert Marcuse, and Jacques Derrida.

Readers should know that some of the very best Freud criticism has been abridged and collected by the now-retired Berkeley literary critic Frederick Crews in *Unauthorized Freud: Doubters Confront a Legend* (1998). Lay readers will be rewarded for examining the twenty contributions, which alone contain, in my opinion, enough scholarship to make anyone rethink psychoanalysis in every aspect. Advanced readers should also see this book, if only for key references to complete works and for other worthwhile references to what I like to call Critical Freud Studies. As for Crews, he is probably best known for his *Memory Wars: Freud's Legacy in Dispute* (1995). This short book, written for mass consumption, contains the essays and angry letters to the editor that first appeared in the *New York Review of Books* (itself once a bastion of proanalytic thought). The book works well in undergraduate classes on Freud, in which the direct and indirect effects of Freudian thought in contemporary society make for lively discussions on everything from false memory to the theory of repression. I recommend it highly. I also recommend a short essay by Crews that perfectly conveys his style and views, "Unconscious Deeps and Empirical Shallows," which appeared in the journal *Philosophy and Literature* (1998). For another look at the legacy of psychoanalysis, this time in the context of academic psychiatry, see Joel Paris's *The Fall of an Icon: Psychoanalysis and Academic Psychiatry* (2005). This accessible book, written by a medical school academic, administrator, and practicing psychiatrist, should be very hard for clinically oriented readers to dismiss as just more Freud bashing among humanities scholars.

Other notable works on the history of psychoanalysis include Richard Webster's comprehensive, earnest examination, *Why Was Freud Wrong: Sin, Science, and Psychoanalysis*, published in 1995. Another is E. M. Thornton's *Freud and Cocaine: The Freudian Fallacy* (1983), the single best work on Freud's early cocaine period. A very good, accessible, and damning source book about Freud's varied impact on the United States is E. Fuller Torrey's *The Freudian Fraud: The Malignant Effect of Freud's Theory on American Thought and Culture* (1992). Essays by Peter Swales are also worth consulting. This independent researcher and enfant terrible is always thought provoking—his interpretations challenging, his humor biting and funny. Beyond that, Swales is a world authority about Freud's life and early patients. Start with his penetrating essays about the prehistory of psychoanalysis, published in volumes 1 and 3 of *Freud: Appraisals and Reappraisals* (1986 and 1988, respectively), edited by Paul Stepansky. For lighter but still impressive fare, see his "Freud, Filthy Lucre, and Undue Influence" published in *Review of Existential Psychology and Psychiatry* (1997).

Readers interested in consulting thoughtful early works on Freud and psychoanalysis should look at Joseph Wortis's *Fragments of an Analysis with Freud* of 1954. Other firsthand accounts include *Freud, Master and Friend* (1945), an unintentionally comical book by Freud's follower Hans Sachs. *Freud as We Knew Him*, edited by Hendrick Ruitenback and published in 1973, is a useful, entirely accessible, often entertaining collection of about sixty personal reflections on Freud by people such as Sachs, Ernest Jones, Andre Breton, Hilida Doolittle (H.D.), Marie Bonaparte, and others. From this book you can trace back to complete texts. Among the newer worthwhile books in this vein, consider Abram Kardiner's *My Analysis with Freud: Reminiscences* (1977), Richard Sterba's *Reminiscences of a Viennese Psychoanalyst* (1982), and Esther Menaker's *Appointment in Vienna: An American Psychoanalyst Recalls Her Student Days in Pre-War Austria* (1989). A more contemporary reassessment based on personal experience can be found in Jeffrey Masson's well-written and accessible *Final Analysis: The Making and Unmaking of a Psychoanalyst* (1990). If you thought that the problems of psychoanalytic training were a thing of the distant past, Masson will set you straight. It is a good book about his life in psychoanalysis.

Of course, an even better source for details about Freud's way of thinking is his vast correspondence. Among the very best is a classic—a work Freud (understandably, in retrospect) wanted to destroy: *The Complete Letters of Sigmund Freud to Wilhelm Fliess, 1887–1904*. Masson brought out the first uncensored edition in 1985. This singular document is essential reading, because with it you hardly need the critics at all to come to wholly skeptical conclusions about psychoanalysis. This book has everything: intrigue about patients, the birth of psychoanalysis, Freud's everyday life, bizarre (and yet familiar, at least to readers of Sulloway) biological speculations, and more. See also Freud's correspondence with Carl Jung (especially for a taste of analytic politics) and with his close friend and analyst, Sandor Ferenczi. In Freud's letters to Ferenczi, he exhibits, well after the birth of psychoanalysis, the same flair for wild metabiological speculation found in his early letters to Fliess.

Two excellent and accessible books on the politics of psychoanalysis are Ernest Gellner's *The Psychoanalytic Movement: The Cunning of Unreason* (1985) and Phyllis Grosskurth's *The Secret Ring: Freud's Inner Circle and the Politics of Psychoanalysis* (1991). The second book is simpler than the first, so choose which one suits you best. An early, but still quite useful, short book on this general subject is Erich Fromm's *Sigmund Freud's Mission* (1959). For a compelling and insightful look at contemporary Freud politics, casual readers can do no better than the *New Yorker* journalist Janet Malcolm's *In the Freud Archives* of 1984. She provides balanced reporting, but readers will probably shake their heads at it all. Read it and then read Masson's reflections of 1990 (see preceding page). Readers will also profit from Adam Gopnik's frank reappraisal of his experience with psychoanalysis as recounted in the *New Yorker* (August 24, and August 31, 1998). For a book-length examination of one woman's experience with psychoanalysis, see Brenda Webster's memoir, *The Last Good Freudian* (2000). It is sometimes frustrating to follow her along, so slow does her realization dawn, but her work is well written and instructive.

If your interest runs toward the politics of French psychoanalysis, then see the expanded second edition of Sherry Turkle's *Psychoanalytic Politics: Jacques Lacan and Freud's French Revolution* (1992). It is well paced and a page turner for those who care. Although written by a partisan commentator, *Jacques Lacan and Co.: A History of Psychoanalysis in France, 1925–1985* (1990) by Elisabeth Roudinesco is equally indispensable on Lacan and the French scene. From a totally different perspective, Borch-Jacobsen's *Lacan: The Absolute Master* (1991) is a devastating demystification of Lacan's thought. I always recommend the masterful first chapter to my upper-year students in philosophy. But, for new readers, perhaps the most accessible introductions to Lacan's thought were written by two advocates: Stuart Schneiderman's *Jacques Lacan: Death of an Intellectual Hero* (1983), a very personal recounting of this English professor's journey into psychoanalysis; and Shoshana Felman's *Jacques Lacan and the Adventure of Insight* (1987), written by a professor of French and comparative literature. A fantastic book that reflects deeply and critically on Lacanian France by reflecting on Freud's life is Roustang's *Dire Mastery: Discipleship from Freud to Lacan* (1982). Roustang was trained as an analyst and apparently still retains a relation to it in his practice; today, however, he is apparently geared more toward hypnosis.

For those who want to consult some classic propsychoanalytic texts, I would immediately recommend the three-volume work that is the standard against which everything else has been measured: Ernest Jones's *The Life and Work of Sigmund Freud* (1953–1957). Jones, an English analyst, outlived Freud's other closest associates and was thus able to spin the early history as it suited him. Note that it can also be found in a more accessible abridged version. Other reverential histories of psychoanalysis include Peter Gay's popular *Freud: A Life for Our Time* (1988) and, more recently, Nathan Hale's two-volume set, *Freud and the Americans* and *The Rise and Crisis of Psychoanalysis in the United States*, published in 1995. Critics complain that these works repeat as fact details we have long known to be fiction, such as the details surrounding the case of Anna O. But readers will certainly find lots of interesting material mixed into the pot.

A recent edited work that assembles like-minded thinkers, many of whom are pro-Freudian, is *The Death of Psychoanalysis: Murder? Suicide? Or Rumor Greatly Exaggerated?* (1999). Readers skeptical about the overall tone of Freud's critics will find solace in at least some of the essays collected here; see, for example, Nathan Hale's attack essay. For a classic attack on Roazen's 221-page *Brother Animal,* see defender of the flame Kurt Eissler's 403-page *Talent and Genius: The Fictitious Case of Tausk Contra Freud* (1971). A great adjudication, albeit one that sides with Roazen, can be found in Roustang's *Dire Mastery.* Those looking to contest the positivistic "arguments" of Sulloway, Masson, and Grünbaum might begin with Paul Robinson's *Freud and His Critics* (1993). Those looking for ammunition against the work of Crews in particular and Freud criticism in general should consider Peter Rudnytsky's "Wrecking Crews" of 1999, published in the journal *American Imago.* Also consider the many angry letters to the editor, along with Crews's detailed responses, that appear in Crews's *Memory Wars.* Those curious about the supposed hate of Freud should see historian Elisabeth Roudinesco's recent book, *Pourquoi Tant De Haine? Anatomie du Livre de la psychoanalyse* (2005). Those seeking a fairly sophisticated apologist for psychoanalysis should look for works by Chicago professor Jonathan Lear. See, for example, his *Open Minded: Working Out the Logic of the Soul* (1998). John Forrester is another sophisticated defender of psychoanalysis; start with his *Dispatches from the Freud Wars* of 1997. His *Seductions of Psychoanalysis: Freud, Lacan, and Derrida* (1990) is also quite interesting and suggests the direction of his interests.

A flurry of letters and articles concerning the controversial Freud exhibit at the Library of Congress were published during the mid-to-late 1990s. You can learn much about recent psychoanalytic politics and culture by reading about this controversy or reviewing the relevant articles and letters themselves. Begin with Michael Roth's *Freud: Conflict and Culture* (2000). For a critical point of view, look at Crews's introduction to *Unauthorized Freud* (1998). You could also consult my short essay collected in the accessible *Killing Freud: Twentieth-Century Culture and the Death of Psychoanalysis* (2003). Alternatively, if you are really ambitious and have lots of time on your hands, you could consult the more than three hundred pages of primary documents that Peter Swales has deposited in the Library of Congress. Note that some materials, such as the original petition signed by critics, can be found online.

For more information about Freud criticism, try googling "Freud bashing" or "Freud bashers." As always, however, buyer beware—the good is mixed in with the ugly. A fantastic general-interest website, one that includes many informed discussions of Freud and psychoanalysis, is Butterflies and Wheels (at butterfliesandwheels.com). Almost as easy, you can just visit the stacks of your library at BF173 and remove books at random. Chances are good that you will immediately find information, much of it woefully out of date, that contradicts what critics say. I'm afraid all this conflicting information makes it very difficult to figure out what you believe, but that's Freud studies. I hope, though, that this short discussion of works in the field can get you started and save you some time and effort. One final rule of thumb for your research always holds: find a book or article, pro- or antipsychoanalytic, and raid its bibliography for other works, like-minded or not.

Readers should also be aware that many documentaries about Freud and psychoanalysis have been made. Most are, in my view, too kind, banal, or both, with the exception of Peter Swales's documentary for a BBC series on "Bad Ideas of the Twentieth Century" called "Freudism." Hilarious, informed, and irreverent, I recommend it highly. Get it if you can. Happy hunting.

References

Borch-Jacobsen, Mikkel. (1988). *The Freudian Subject*, trans. Catherine Porter. Stanford, CA: Stanford University Press.

———. 1991. *Lacan: The Absolute Master*, trans. Douglas Brick. Stanford, CA: University of Stanford Press.

———. 1993. *The Emotional Tie: Psychoanalysis, Mimesis, and Affect*, trans. D. Brick and others. Stanford, CA: Stanford University Press.

———. 1996. *Remembering Anna O.: A Century of Mystification*, trans. K. Olson, X. Callahan, and M. Borch-Jacobsen. New York: Routledge.

———. 1997. "The Making and Marketing of a Disease: An Interview with Herbert Spiegel," in *Freud Under Analysis: History, Theory, Practice*, ed. T. Dufresne. Northvale, NJ: Jason Aronson.

Bruner, Jerome. 1973. "Freud and the Image of Man," in *Freud: Modern Judgements*, ed. F. Cioffi. London: Macmillan.

Cioffi, Frank, ed. 1973. *Freud: Modern Judgements*. London: Macmillan.

———. 1998a. *Freud and the Question of Pseudoscience*. Chicago: Open Court.

———. 1998b. "The Freud Controversy: What Is at Issue?" in *Freud: Conflict and Culture*, ed. M. Roth. New York: Knopf.

———. 1998c. *Wittgenstein on Freud and Frazer*. Cambridge: Cambridge University Press.

Cohen, I. Bernard. 1985. "Transformation of Scientific Ideas," in *Revolution in Science*. London: Harvard University Press.

Crews, Frederick. 1966. *The Sins of the Fathers: Hawthorne's Psychological Themes*. New York: Oxford University Press.

———. 1986. *Skeptical Engagements*. New York: Oxford University Press.

———. 1992. *The Critics Bear It Away: American Fiction and the Academy*. New York: Random House.

———. 1995. *The Memory Wars: Freud's Legacy in Dispute*. New York: New York Review.

———. ed. 1998. *Unauthorized Freud: Doubters Confront a Legend*. New York: Viking.

Darwin, Charles. 1958. *The Autobiography of Charles Darwin, 1809–1882*, ed. N. Barlow. New York: Norton.

Doolittle, Hilda. 1974. *Tribute to Freud.* Boston: Godine.

Dufresne, Todd. 2000. *Tales from the Freudian Crypt: The Death Drive in Text and Context*, foreword by M. Borch-Jacobsen. Stanford, CA: Stanford University Press.

———. 2003. *Killing Freud: Twentieth-Century Culture and the Death of Psychoanalysis.* London: Continuum.

———. 2004. "Psychoanalysis Is Dead . . . So How Does That Make You Feel?" *Los Angeles Times*, February 18.

Eagle, Morris. 1998. [Untitled]. *Contemporary Psychology*, 33 (5).

Ellenberger, Henri. 1970. *The Discovery of the Unconscious: The History and Evolution of Dynamic Psychiatry.* New York: Basic Books.

Esterson, Allen 1993. *Seductive Mirage: An Exploration of the Work of Sigmund Freud.* Chicago: Open Court.

———. 1996. "Grünbaum's Tally Argument." *History of the Human Sciences*, 9 (1): 43–57.

———. 1998. "Jeffrey Masson and Freud's Seduction Theory: A New Fable Based on Old Myths." *History of the Human Sciences*, 11(1): 1–21.

———. 2001. "The Mythologizing of Psychoanalytic History: Deception and Self-Deception in Freud's Accounts of the Seduction Theory Episode." *History of Psychiatry*, 12: 329–352.

———. 2002. "The Myth of Freud's Ostracism by the Medical Community in 1896–1905: Jeffrey Masson's Assault on Truth." *History of Psychology*, 5 (2): 115–134.

Fliess, Wilhelm. 1897. *Die Beziehungen zwischen Nase und weiblichen Geschlechtsorganen: In ihrer biologischen Bedeutung dargestellt.* Vienna: Franz Deuticke.

Freud, Sigmund. 1895. "Project for a Scientific Psychology," *Standard Edition of the Complete Psychological Works of Sigmund Freud* (SE), ed. James Strachey. London: Hogarth Press, 1953–1974, vol. 1: 281–397.

———. 1896. "The Aetiology of Hysteria," SE vol. 3: 189–221.

———. 1899. "Screen Memories," SE vol. 3: 301–322.

———. 1900. *The Interpretation of Dreams*, SE vols. 4 & 5.

———. 1901. *The Psychopathology of Everyday Life*, SE vol. 6.

———. 1905. *Three Essays on the Theory of Sexuality*, SE vol. 7: 123–243.

———. 1911. "Psychoanalytic Notes on an Autobiographical Account of a Case of Paranoia," SE vol. 12: 1–82.

———. 1911–1915. "Papers on Technique," SE vol. 12: 85–173.

———. 1913. *Totem and Taboo*, SE vol. 13: 1–161.

———. 1915. "A Case of Paranoia Running Counter to the Psychoanalytic Theory of the Disease," SE vol. 14: 261–272.

———. 1916–1917. *Introductory Lectures on Psychoanalysis*, SE vols. 15, 16.

———. 1920. *Beyond the Pleasure Principle*, SE vol. 18: 7–64.

———. 1921. *Group Psychology and the Analysis of the Ego,* SE vol. 19: 65–143.

———. 1923. *The Ego and the Id*, SE vol. 19: 1–66.

———. 1926. *The Question of Lay Analysis*, SE vol. 20: 179–258.

———. 1927. *The Future of an Illusion*, SE vol. 21: 1–56.

———. 1930. *Civilization and Its Discontents*, SE vol. 21: 64–145.

———. 1937. "Analysis Terminable and Interminable," SE vol. 23: 211–253.

———. 1939. *Moses and Monotheism*, SE vol. 23: 139–207.

———. 1974. *Cocaine Papers*, notes by Anna Freud, ed. Robert Byck. New York: Stonehill.

———, and Josef Breuer. 1893–1895. *Studies on Hysteria*, SE vol. 2.

———, and Sandor Ferenczi. 1993. *The Correspondence of Sigmund Freud and Sandor Ferenczi, vol. 1: 1908–1914*, ed. E. Brabant, E. Falzeder, P. Giampieri-Deutsch; trans. P. T. Hoffer. Cambridge, MA: Harvard University Press.

———, and Wilhelm Fliess. 1985. *The Complete Letters of Sigmund Freud to Wilhelm Fliess, 1887–1904*, ed. Jeffrey M. Masson. Cambridge, MA: Harvard University Press.

———, and Carl Jung. 1974. *The Freud/Jung Letters: The Correspondence Between Sigmund Freud and C. G. Jung*, ed. W. McGuire, trans. R. Manheim and R. F. C. Hull. Cambridge, MA: Harvard University Press.

Gardner, Muriel (ed). 1971. *The Wolf-Man and Sigmund Freud*. New York: Basic Books.

Gay, Peter. 1988. *Freud: A Life for Our Time*. New York: Norton.

Gibbs, W. 1955. "A Couch of My Own." *New Yorker*, February 19: 29–30.

Glover, Edward. 1952. "Research Methods and Psychoanalysis." *International Journal of Psychoanalysis*, 33: 403–409.

Gosling, Francis G. 1987. *Before Freud: Neurasthenia and the American Medical Community, 1870–1910*. Urbana: University of Illinois Press.

Grosskurth, Phyllis. 1980. *Havelock Ellis: A Biography*. Toronto: McClelland and Steward.

Grünbaum, Adolf. 1984. *The Foundations of Psychoanalysis: A Philosophical Critique*. Berkeley: University of California Press.

Hale, Jr., Nathan. 1999. "Freud's Critics: A Critical Look." *Partisan Review*, 66(2): 235–254.

Hirschmüller, Albrecht. 1989. *The Life and Work of Josef Breuer: Physiology and Psychoanalysis*. New York: New York University Press.

Israëls, Han. 1989. *Schreber: Father and Son*. Madison, CT: International Universities Press.

———, and Morton Schatzman. 1993. "The Seduction Theory." *History of Psychiatry*, 4 (March): 23–59.

Horgan, John. 1996a. *The End of Science: Facing the Limits of Knowledge in the Twilight of the Scientific Age*. Reading, MA: Addison-Wesley.

———. 1996b. "Why Freud Isn't Dead." *Scientific American*, 12: 74–79.

———. 1999. *The Undiscovered Mind: How the Human Mind Defies Replication, Medication, and Explanation*. New York: Free Press.

James, William. 1890. *Principles of Psychology*, with intro. by George A. Miller. Cambridge, MA: Harvard University Press [1983].

Jones, Ernest. 1953–1957. *The Life and Works of Sigmund Freud, 1856–1939*. 3 vols. New York: Basic Books.

Kraupl-Taylor, F. 1987. Editorial. *Psychological Medicine*, 17: 557–560.

Kuhn, Thomas. 1962. *The Structure of Scientific Revolutions*. Chicago: University of Chicago Press

Lear, Jonathan. 1995. "The Shrink Is In: A Counterblast in the War on Freud," *New Republic*, December 25: 18–25.

Löwenfeld, Leopold. 1899. *Sexualleben und Nervenleiden: Die nervösen Störungen sexuellen Ursprungs*. Wiesbaden: J. F. Bergmann.

Macmillan, Malcolm. 1997. *Freud Evaluated: The Completed Arc*, foreword by F. Crews. Cambridge, MA: MIT Press.

Masson, Jeffrey Moussaieff. 1984. *The Assault on Truth: Freud's Suppression of the Seduction Theory*. New York: HarperCollins.

———, ed. 1985. *The Complete Letters of Sigmund Freud to Wilhelm Fliess, 1887–1904*. Cambridge, MA: Harvard University Press.

Menaker, Esther. 1979. *Masochism and the Emergent Ego*. New York: Human Sciences Press.

———. 1982. *Otto Rank: A Rediscovered Legacy*. New York: Columbia University Press.

———. 1989. *Appointment in Vienna: An American Psychoanalyst Recalls Her Student Days in Pre-War Austria*. New York: St. Martin's Press.

———. 1996. *Separation, Will, and Creativity: The Wisdom of Otto Rank*. Northvale, NJ: Jason Aronson Press

Menaker, Esther, and William Menaker. 1965. *Ego and Evolution*. New York: Grove Press.

Merton, Robert K. 1976. "The Ambivalence of Scientists," in *Sociological Ambivalence and Other Essays*. New York: Free Press.

Meyer, Catherine, with Mikkel Borch-Jacobsen, Jean Cottraux, Didier Pleux, and Jacques Van Rillaer. 2005. *Le livre noir de la psychanalyse: vivre, penser et aller mieux sans Freud* [The Black Book of Psychoanalysis: How to Live, Think, and Get on Better Without Freud]. Paris: Arènes.

Nagel, Thomas. 1994. "Freud's Permanent Revolution." *New York Review of Books,* May 12: 34–38.

Niederland, William. 1984. *The Schreber Case: The Psychoanalytic Profile of a Paranoid Personality,* expanded ed. Hillsdale, NJ: Analytic Press.

Nietzsche, Friedrich. 1888. *Twilight of the Idols: Or, How One Philosophizes with a Hammer,* in *The Portable Nietzsche,* ed. Walter Kaufmann. New York: Penguin, 1954.

Oakley, Chris. 1997. "Basta Così! Mikkel Borch-Jacobsen on Psychoanalysis and Philosophy," in *Returns of the "French Freud": Freud, Lacan, and Beyond,* ed. T. Dufresne. New York: Routledge.

Obholzer, Karin. 1982. *The Wolf-Man Sixty Years Later: Conversations with Freud's Controversial Patient.* London: Routledge and Kegan Paul.

Roazen, Paul. 1975. *Freud and His Followers.* New York: Knopf.

Rosenthal, Robert. 1966. *Experimenter Effects in Behavioral Research.* New York: Appleton-Century-Crofts.

Roudinesco, Elisabeth. 1986. *La Bataille de cent ans: histoire de la psychoanalyse,* vol. 1, 2nd ed. Paris: Le Seuil.

Roustang, Francois. 1983. *Psychoanalysis Never Lets Go,* trans. N. Lukacher. Baltimore: Johns Hopkins University Press.

Schatzman, Morton. 1973. *Soul Murder: Persecution in the Family.* New York: New American Library.

———. 1980. *The Story of Ruth.* New York: Putnam.

Schimek, Jean G. 1987. "Fact and Fantasy in the Seduction Theory: A Historical Review." *Journal of the American Psychoanalytic Association,* 35: 937–965.

Schreber, Daniel Paul. 1998. *Memoirs of My Nervous Illness,* trans. and ed. I. Macalpine and R. Hunter. Cambridge, MA: Harvard University Press. (Orig. German pub. 1903.)

Shamdasani, Sonu. 1998. *Cult Fictions: C. G. Jung and the Founding of Analytical Psychology.* London: Routledge.

———. 2003. *Jung and the Making of Modern Psychology: The Dream of a Science.* Cambridge: Cambridge University Press.

Sharpe, Ellen Freeman. 1937. *Dream Analysis.* London: Hogarth.

Shorter, Edward. 1985. *Bedside Manners: The Troubled History of Doctors and Patients.* New York: Simon & Schuster.

———. 1992. *From Paralysis to Fatigue: A History of Psychosomatic Illness in the Modern Era.* New York: Free Press.

———. 1994. *From the Mind into the Body: The Cultural Origins of Psychosomatic Symptoms.* New York: Free Press.

———. 1997a. *A History of Psychiatry: From the Era of the Asylum to the Age of Prozac.* New York: John Wiley.

———. 1997b. "What Was the Matter with Anna O.: A Definitive Analysis," in *Freud Under Analysis: History, Theory, Practice,* ed. T. Dufresne. Northvale, NJ: Jason Aronson.

———. 2005a. *A Historical Dictionary of Psychiatry.* Oxford: Oxford University Press.

———. 2005b. *Written in the Flesh: A History of Desire.* Toronto: University of Toronto Press.

Simon, William, and John Gagnon. 1974. "On Psychosexual Development," in *Clues to the Riddle of Man,* ed. W. Graham and R. Lazarus. New York: Prentice Hall.

Stannard, David E. 1980. *Shrinking History.* New York: Oxford University Press.

Sulloway, Frank. 1979. *Freud, Biologist of the Mind: Beyond the Psychoanalytic Legend.* New York: Basic Books.

———. 1992. "Reassessing Freud's Case Histories: The Social Construction of Psychoanalysis," in *Freud and the History of Psychoanalysis,* ed. T. Gelfand and J. Kerr. Hillsdale, NJ: Analytic Press.

———. 1996. *Born to Rebel: Birth Order, Family Dynamics, and Creative Lives.* New York: Vintage.

Swales, Peter. 1989. "Freud, Fliess, and Fratricide: The Role of Fliess in Freud's Conception of Paranoia," in *Sigmund Freud: Critical Assessments,* vol. 1, ed. L. Spurling. London: Routledge.

Thornton, E. M. 1983. *Freud and Cocaine: The Freudian Fallacy.* London: Blond & Briggs.

Weisz, George. 1975. "Scientists and Sectarians: The Case of Psychoanalysis." *Journal of the History of the Behavioral Sciences,* 11: 350–64.

Wittgenstein, Ludwig. 1980. *Culture and Value.* Oxford: Blackwell.

Wittels, Fritz. 1924. *Sigmund Freud: His Personality, His Teaching, and His School,* trans. E. Paul and C. Paul. London: George Allen & Unwin.

Wortis, Joseph. 1940. "Fragments of a Freudian Analysis." *American Journal of Orthopsychiatry,* 10: 843–849.

———. 1950. *Soviet Psychiatry.* Baltimore: Williams & Wilkins.

———. 1954. *Fragments of an Analysis with Freud.* Repr. New York: J. Aronson, 1985.

Index